LUST

ANGER

UNDERSTANDING SEXUAL ADDICTION
and the
ROAD TO HEALTHY INTIMACY

Love

MAUREEN CANNING, MA, LMFT

SOURCEBOOKS, INC.®
NAPERVILLE, ILLINOIS

Published by Sourcebooks, Inc.
P.O. Box 4410, Naperville, Illinois 60567-4410
(630) 961-3900
Fax: (630) 961-2168
www.sourcebooks.com

Library of Congress Cataloging-in-Publication Data

Canning, Maureen.
  Lust, anger, and love : understanding sexual addiction and the road
to healthy intimacy / Maureen Canning.
    p. cm.
  ISBN-13: 978-1-4022-0868-3 (pbk.)
  ISBN-10: 1-4022-0868-5 (pbk.)
  1. Sex addiction. I. Title.

RC560.S43C36 2008
616.85'83—dc22

                                         2007029512

Printed and bound in the United States of America.
VP 10 9 8 7 6 5 4 3 2 1

This Book Is Dedicated to All Who Still Suffer

We are going to know a new freedom and a new happiness.... We will comprehend the word serenity and know we will know peace.

—*Twelve Steps of Alcoholics Anonymous*

CONTENTS

ACKNOWLEDGMENTS

This book is a labor of love. It is born out of a passion that has been influenced by many situations and many individuals throughout my life, the first being my sisters. They are my touchstones to the past and a constant reminder of the courage of the spirit. The clients with whom I have had the honor of working have had an immeasurable influence on this book. The gift of their vulnerability and trust serves as a constant reminder of the possibility of the healing process. Patrick Carnes, an early mentor of mine, was the first to write about sexual addiction as a disorder. His early work serves as the foundation of my clinical practice. Pia Mellody, who pioneered models of codependency and love addiction, has been both a supportive colleague and a friend.

I want to thank Larry Fruendlich, without whom this book would have not been possible. His knowledge and belief in the project guided me through this process from its inception to its final draft. He has been both a creative partner and an advocate of this work. Loretta Barrett, my agent, believed in the importance of this book's message, and stalwartly guided this project to its completion. Hillel Black, my editor, whose steady, gentle tutelage and guidance pushed my creative edge, was the overseer of the big picture, the architect to its final end.

I would like to thank Claudia Black and Jack Fahey, who have been good friends and supportive colleagues; Elizabeth Griffin, who has been with me since the beginning, and is not only a trusted colleague but also a loving friend; and Marsha Rusby, whose encouragement, love, and affirmations have been a true gift and a cornerstone in my life.

I would like to thank my husband and best friend Bob Fulton, whose love and partnership have been the most gratifying, rewarding, and enriching relational experience of my life. Each day he reminds me of what goodness is and gives me the gift of his precious being.

Last, I would like to thank those in the recovering community who touched my life. Your courage, strength, and hope were the beacon that led me out of my darkness. It is for those who have yet to find the light, those who still suffer in their addictions, that I write this book. I hold for you the hope and promise I was given when I began this journey.

Oh, maker of mine,
Oh, weaver of truth,
How harsh is the history.
How foul is the curse.
I come empty-handed
As lonely as death.
The wretched, vile toxins
That ooze without regret.
A broken spirit, a pitiful wench
Lacking illumination, luster and spent.
This poor little waif of terror and fear
Trapped in a mirror of shattered segments.
There in the darkness lies a beacon of light
Like fire and water of earthly delight.
Carving and etching with painstaking care,
A maker of truth with each uncovered layer.
Oh, agony of mine,
Oh, lancer of pain,
How I trust in thy goodness,
Letting go not in vain.
Begging and pleading with each unanswered prayer,
With only witness and teacher to care.
Like a spot of blood in the fresh-fallen snow,
A soul so defiled and miracles that unfold.
Emergence of spirit, redeemer of soul,
How grateful and humbled is that of old.
A teacher, a healer of promise, of faith,
Now with redemption and embracing of grace.

—*Maureen Canning*

AUTHOR TO READER

Sex is one of the most powerful forces in the human condition. It can drive individuals to the pinnacle of emotional and physical ecstasy or, conversely, spiral other people into depths of despair and anguish. The power of sexual energy and expression exists because our sexuality is tied, or connected, to the core of who we are; it is our essence, our life force, our creativity, and our passion.

A sense of self means an inner knowing, a clarity of our true nature or authenticity. In healthy sexual expression, there is desire, connection, and a sense of well-being. The act of expressing one's self sexually results in a positive, life-enhancing experience; it is an expression of love, an exchange of mutual pleasuring and respect that leads to an intimate connection.

The sexual compulsive person may think this is what he or she is experiencing. However, the opposite is true. Sex for the addict is about intensity, danger, power, and control. It is about emotional numbing, conquering, and getting high. Sex becomes a commodity to be manipulated, a means to a self-defeating end. Sex and love become a game to play, an avoidance, a push/pull, or a hunger so powerful that the addict will risk everything to reach that sexual high.

No risk or consequence has stopped the addict: disease, financial ruin, lost relationships, legal injunctions, career setbacks, or self-respect. The addict is caught in an intoxicating dance that has induced a delusional reality.

This is the cycle of sex addiction, and it is deadly—not always in physical form, but most assuredly in emotional experience. This "soul" death is temporarily allayed when the addict is on the "hunt" for sex or, at the other extreme, is avoiding sex at all costs. At either end of the spectrum, the addict feels in control and powerful. This is the high, a chemical release that is as addicting as any drug. When these chemicals—or the high—are induced, euphoria washes over the addict, creating the illusion of complete immunity to the realities of his or her internal ache.

Sexual addiction is not a moral issue; it is a coping mechanism born out of the addict's wounding. The types of wounding can be as diverse as the addicts themselves. Not all addicts are aware of their "wounding," as abuse or trauma is often covert. When a person is wounded or traumatized, he or she must learn to cope, often without understanding or support. In order to cope or escape their painful realities, addicts may use drugs, alcohol, food, shopping, staying busy, controlling others, or work. Sex addicts escape through sex.

Like a steamroller, they cover, protect, and seal the layers of their painful past. Unfortunately, the layers are never erased. The history is embedded like sediments layered in a canyon wall, linear markings of a sordid history, buried but never forgotten.

All sex addicts are profoundly angry at the people they think they love or to whom they have the greatest attraction. Sexual lust or fantasy is the result of the addiction. However, anger is its driving force. Sexualized anger attempts to hide or bury the shame addicts feel at their core. When I suggest to a client (let's say he is a heterosexual male) that he is angry at women, his response may be, "What are you talking about? Angry at women? I love women! I seek them out! I want to have sex with all the women in the world!"

After listening to this, I ask, "Do you love your wife?"

"Of course I love my wife. She's the mother of my children."

"Well, how have you treated her?"

"Oh, not very well."

"Have you lied to her?"

"Yeah."

"Did you betray her trust? How have you treated your mistress?"

"Well. It's been a pretty rocky road."

"Have you lied to her and humiliated her?"

"Well, that's her side of the story. . . ."

And so it goes on, with me pointing out all of his behaviors that demonstrate that, rather than loving his wife, girlfriend, or mistress, he treats them with anger.

Women are equally blocked in identifying their anger toward the men with whom they are emotionally involved. They, too, do not want to hear how angry their emotional vulnerability makes them.

In my practice, I continually see how sexual anger is generated by shame. Not just the shame of people acting against their values—but the shame that tells people that, at the core or deepest parts of their being, they feel worthless and inadequate. Living in shame is an uncomfortable place for addicts because shame generates feelings of being less valuable than others, being vulnerable, or being out of control. To combat these feelings, the addict uses anger as the cure. Anger allows the addict to move from feeling vulnerable to feeling "safe." Anger acts as a mask or a wall the addict can hide behind—he may feel safer, but it is a lonely, isolated place to live. Often the addict lives between these two extremes: the low of shame and the high of anger.

My work as a therapist specializing in sexual compulsivity leads me to search for the connection between that early shaming/wounding and a sexual component, that is, a specific incident in which sex and shame got connected. All my work as a sexual compulsivity therapist ultimately depends on nurturing my clients to an understanding of how their childhood shame developed this sexual or eroticized component. The yoking together of sexual energy under conditions of severe abuse creates traumatic connections that, in later life, will associate sex with shame, pain, and anger. I call the resulting product of this pathological association *sexualized anger*. Recognizing it in the lives of my clients—and coaching them to remake their emotional lives, free from shame-based sexual compulsion—may be the most essential part of my work.

In my practice, I am continually blessed by witnessing the transformation of my clients from the hopelessness of the sexual addictive cycle to the self-empowerment of healthy sexual expression. In the healing process, I see how the ravages of sexual addiction whittle away any sense of well-being and emotional health. The undying courage to heal these wounds can lead the recovering addict on an arduous path. However, it is a path of unimaginable rewards.

I say this from both my professional experience and my own personal healing journey, a journey that led me to my own discovery of my original wounding.

Chapter 1

MY OWN STORY OF SEXUALIZED ANGER

ONE

I am sitting in my car, stuck behind a San Francisco MUNY electric bus on Market Street. My months in the tree-lined suburbs have made me vulnerable to the horrors of downtown traffic. I watch as the conductor tediously repositions the electrical power arm that has been jostled off the track high above his head. He annoys me, and so does the stupid electrical system. I am trapped between hostile traffic and the fear and frustration that live deep within me.

In the suffocating cocoon of my non-air-conditioned, '84 diesel Mercedes, I wonder about this journey I am embarking upon. The irritating knocking of the diesel engine and the stifling air intensify my insecurities. I think of how my sweat-stained armpits will embarrass me in front of the people I want to impress. I glance at the clock, worried not only about my appearance, but about my tardiness as well.

Only two weeks earlier, I had read an article in the *San Francisco Chronicle* about a revolutionary program to reform first-time solicitors of prostitutes. My eyes darted to the bottom of the page to find the contact numbers. I called immediately and volunteered my services.

The men I was about to meet had violated the law in pursuit of psychosexual needs that were oblivious to danger and social consequences. One hundred of them would be sitting in front of me, doing penance and/or seeking understanding and relief. But the tales of the male perpetrators were not my primary interest; it was the stories of the women they had used, who had sold their bodies to nameless faces. They would tell their stories, and what I wanted to hear, above all, was how they had crawled out from the darkness.

I am now honking as the sweat pours down my face. I am distracted by a motorcycle in my rearview mirror. The driver is weaving in and out of traffic. "Jesus Christ," I mutter to myself, "that guy almost hit me."

As I continue down Market Street, I realize I am in parts of the city I have never visited—seedy, dirty, and repulsive. I see the homeless, dressed in stained rags, pushing shopping carts. What would it be like to live on the street, to have no home and no food, to be forced to sell my body? I was once told that pain is pain, but I can't help but wonder: Do I know the suffering of the women I am about to meet? Do I see my pain reflected here on this street corner? Do I know what it is like to hear the clicking of high heels as I maneuver to turn a trick? Do

I know the smell of the "john," the man I sell my body to, as I rock to the rhythm of his pelvis?

It is grim, but, at the same time, this seedy underbelly of life fascinates me. How do women reach this point of degradation, and where does it end? I am hoping to find some of those answers today, to look into the lives of those women called "soiled doves," those hardened females who hold tight to the johns' secrets, and even tighter to their own.

Traffic has freed up, and, as the road rises, the neighborhood improves. Gone are the dirt and ragtag stench. I see increasingly affluent homes nestled on the hillside. My diesel does her best to take the winding hill, affording a cool breeze, the smell of eucalyptus, and an incredible view.

I am feeling calmer until I realize that I have just passed my turn. I had anticipated that the Police Academy would be in a rundown neighborhood, in keeping with the sordidness of its clientele. Nice shopping area, nice condo. It is jarring, the juxtaposition of these two worlds colliding on this hill.

As I make my turn, descending, I see the Academy, a large institutional facility set among large trees with views overlooking the city. The parking lot is empty except for a few cars lined up in front of the biggest building. Pulling into a parking space, I feel my anxiety rising, when I am distracted by the loud squeak of a car door and the sound of laughter. The squeak comes from a decrepit old Ford, the fender dented, the windows filthy, the paint fading. I see two women get out of the car. From a distance, I can't make out their faces. They seem young and jovial but, as they move, it is as if a weight bends their shoulders and drags at their feet.

I sit and watch, wondering how to approach them in order to learn from their lives. Does my own history of pain or my current course of studies justify my curiosity, or will they think that I am a voyeur?

My too-rapid steps and shallow breathing remind me to contain my nervous energy. But the pounding of my heart drowns out these thoughts. As I approach the two women, I thrust out my hand to one in an overly confident manner, and we lock eyes.

The two pools of darkness, in which I instantly imagine volumes of rare and powerful experiences, startle me. I feel humbled and caught off guard. I introduce myself in a manner better suited for the director of the Junior League than for a participant in a criminal sex offenders' program.

Ignoring my extended hand, she bends over and retrieves from her backseat a tattered cardboard box overflowing with material.

"Um hmm. I'm Norma," she grunts, hitting the top of the doorframe, dropping half of the contents onto the concrete.

"Oh, hi," I say, my enthusiasm spilling over, much like the contents of Norma's brimming box. Once Norma is upright, the other woman shoots her a look of exasperation and whisks by me.

I press on.

"I know that I am not presenting until second-to-last, but I thought I would get here early to hear the whole program."

Norma is less than impressed as she closes the squeaky door of her car.

I say, "I have brought books and reference material, so I will go and get them from my car; just tell me where we will be meeting."

"Umm," Norma grunts again, walking right past me.

"We'll be in through those doors," she says, inclining her head in the direction of the building.

As I turn my back and walk to my car, I feel heaviness set in. The view of the city is now obscured by the fog bank that settles in like my mood.

The room is large. Men are taking their seats on the hard metal folding chairs. Norma is busy unloading her material while she talks with a large man in a cheap, tight suit. I notice the second woman from the parking lot talking with a few other women. I gather my courage to approach Norma. She tells me where to put my stuff and to take a seat in the back. Her tone is dismissive, detached, and cold. I sense that she doesn't care about me, and I feel diminished.

The men are of all ages and races. They are quiet as they await an eight-hour day of instruction. If they are successful and finish the course, they can expunge this from their record—this first-time arrest for solicitation of a prostitute.

Norma is making her way to the front of the room. But with the rustling of papers, squeaking of chairs, and murmurs from the crowd, introductions and instructions are barely audible until a commanding woman, the district attorney, rattles off the remainder of information for the daily schedule. The health department, the prostitutes, an intervention plan for sexual addiction, and the irate neighborhoods are on the lineup for the day's agenda. The room quiets down as the area's residents are invited to begin the daily proceedings.

"These are our neighborhoods, our homes."

"You are disgusting, dirty."

"Think about our families, our children. We see you. We see what you are doing. We used to look away, but no more. This has got to stop."

"My children see you doing it outside their bedroom window. My children find condoms on sidewalks. My children have to walk past the pushers and pimps. Does your family have to deal with this in your neighborhood?"

There is little response from the men. The energy in the room is heavy, as if the shame they feel has been carried for decades, alongside lost love, lost childhoods, lost selves. I realize that they are acting out a compulsive ritual. They don't care about children. They don't care about families. They don't care about anything but their fix, their sexual high. They don't care what or whom it costs.

I have come to believe that it is a longing to find love, or the illusion of love, that drives these men to the street, where they use sex as the elixir to soothe their pain.

I am saddened by the irate anger of the neighbors, although I understand it. The neighborhood residents would not say these things if they understood the self-hate and the inescapable shame of the perpetrators. "Never again," these sex addicts tell themselves. "Never again will I put myself at risk. Never will I come to this neighborhood and act out my perverse fantasies." But those "never agains" last only until the next urge.

As the room empties, Norma introduces me to Lieutenant Dutto.

"I have known Norma for years," the Lieutenant explains.

"I used to be the arresting officer in vice crimes when she was working the streets," he says, chuckling.

The large man I had seen earlier is no longer intimidating; his face has softened, and his smile is warm.

"Yeah, Norma was one of our regulars back in those days. We arrested her more than a couple hundred times. I never would have believed she'd turn her life around," he says with pride, as if he had mentored her transformation.

As she listens, Norma's locked jaw and chiseled face soften, and she gives him a knowing smile. There is a bond between them.

As we are talking, a tall, big-breasted blonde in a very short, black skirt joins our circle and is introduced as one of the department's "decoys," a female officer who poses as a prostitute.

Earlier, I had noticed her talking with some of the johns, laughing and joking. It seemed strange: the friendly, light-hearted banter between the hunter and the prey.

The hour-long break feels like a lifetime while I await the startup of the afternoon session. As the men settle in, Norma begins.

"There is an ugly truth out there on the street. It is not glamorous. These women do not make money. They are usually in a stable controlled by a pimp. In the stable, there is a pecking order. The senior women are beaten less. The new girls are beaten daily. Beaten for anything: for taking too long with a customer, showing up late, complaining, lying.

"Most of these girls are tired, sick, but the pimp doesn't care. All he wants is the money and, if he doesn't get it, they get beat. At the end of the day, all they have to show for their work is a black eye and some bruises.

"The women you are about to meet are here to tell you their stories. They are here to share with you the realities of their lives. Most of these women did not intend to end up on the street. No one does. They got hooked and barely broke free."

Norma speaks with conviction, focus, and determination. Once a medical technician, Norma got hooked on drugs and, by the end, was shooting up six times a day. She turned her first trick at twenty-eight.

She is most proud of her recovery and of the SISTERS program she helped to establish. Through the San Francisco County jails, SISTERS has helped women get out of prostitution. "Each and every one of these women is a walking miracle," Norma says with pride.

Norma also founded SAGE (Standing against Global Exploitation), an organization dedicated to helping prostitutes get off the street. There is no break as Norma introduces the women, all graduates of the SISTERS program.

"I felt dead," one of the graduates begins, addressing the men in the room. "When I was out there on the street, and when you wanted to turn a trick, I was completely numb.

All I knew was I hated you and used you to vent my anger. You weren't a person. You were an object, a way to get my drugs, and I couldn't have cared less. You had no face. You had no name. I told you what you wanted to hear, did what you wanted me to do, and died a little more each time."

Her voice is gravelly, her body taut, her eyes glued to the floor. Perhaps she'd been a beauty at one time, but life on the street has eroded the traces of that beauty.

"I was from a white upper-class neighborhood," the second woman says. "I was in college going for a degree in design and got hooked on speed, mostly from staying up late studying. I needed more and more dope and ended up on the street to pay for my habit."

There are no traces left of that suburban life. She, too, is hardened and edgy.

"I'd get more money if you didn't use a condom," she continues. "I'd lie right to your face, saying you were the only one I ever did this with. I just wanted your money to get drugs. You guys were so stupid to believe me, because it was all a big game."

"I was molested by my uncle," the petite third woman begins in a soft voice. "He used to tie me up and rape me when I was twelve years old. I was scared shitless, but I never let him know. On the street, I used to act that shit out, tie guys in up in the closet, have sex with them, and then leave them in there for hours. They became my pets; I did whatever I wanted to them. I got to vent my anger and feel in control," she adds with a sigh that collapses her chest, as if telling her story has drained the life out of her.

"Each of us is off the street, clean, and sober," Norma

continues. "For me, I had to plead with a judge to lock me up. He told me to go home, but I had no home. I knew that if I went back out, I'd end up dead. I went off drugs cold turkey, and I got lucky when I met an ex-whore–turned–social worker who helped me get clean. Not all of us are so lucky."

The room is quiet as the men disperse for their break. I wonder whether they are touched, or are they detached behind a wall of denial?

As Norma comes back to the room, she tells me that I will be up next. Feeling very small next to her, I muster a smile.

"Your story was very moving."

"Yeah," she says, half-smirking, indifferent to my comment.

I am greeted with a sea of eyes. Some of them seem interested, most of them bored. I tune out Norma's introduction as I reflect on what has brought me here. A quote from Elie Wiesel runs through my head: "Let us remember, what hurts the victim most is not the cruelty of the oppressor, but the silence of the bystander."

Perhaps that is why I am here: to have a voice. I, too, have known pain, lived through it, and survived. But I still question whether I am entitled to it, as if measuring my voice against a superlative of suffering to which my own does not compare. I have never been arrested nor had venereal disease. I have never been in jail or shot up drugs. I have never been a prostitute in a pimp's stable.

But I can relate to the eyes I meet and the stories I hear

because I, too, have been sold—not on the street, but by my own mother, who turned away when the abuse began and who remained silent during all the years that followed.

Two

On the outside, it was an idyllic life. We lived in middle-class Nirvana: tree-lined streets, barbeques on Sundays, Barbies in the backyard, kickball in the front. We caught fireflies as the sun set. We spent warm summer nights on our grandparents' farm, and, when it turned cold, we built snowmen on the hill and drank hot chocolate by the fire. It wasn't until the lights went off that the secret life began.

Late at night, in the basement, where my father stole my virginity and raped my soul, I learned how to hate my body, my sex, and all that was to become *me*. My abuse began before I could speak. Too young to comprehend what was happening to my body, I was able only to sense the physical violation and the despair.

My father's father was orphaned in his formative years, and, having no family to take him in, he spent the remainder of his childhood at a boarding house. My father's mother, an Italian immigrant, was living in tents at age thirteen, outside the city limits in a rural town in western Missouri.

I remember my shock when I first saw the pictures: hundreds of tents lined up like on a military base. Women adorned in faded dresses, men in worn overalls. They stood in mud up to their ankles, their expressions dull and lifeless.

My father's father joined the Navy as soon as he was of age, and, when he returned from World War I, he became a miner in the Missouri hills. Those caverns were known to swallow men or blacken their lungs, but my grandfather survived. He married my grandmother, eventually bought a farm, and produced three boys, my father being the youngest.

My father's childhood, although markedly better than that of his parents, was dominated by deprivation and hardship. He endured having to work at relentless chores even before the light of day, plus snowstorms on his three-mile walk to the schoolhouse. The physical exertions took their toll—as did the emotional abuse, doled out more from ignorance than from intent. His parents were neither demonstrative nor loving. They learned and lived the bare, cold existence of survival—a life lacking emotional connection, something my father needed and longed for. The devastating effect of this abuse was a void in my father's soul, an ache so deep that he would never know emotional peace. His mother was loud, domineering, and controlling—a defense masking the anxiety of her own troubled youth. Her father was withdrawn, absent, and alcoholic.

My father had wit and intelligence but, like his father, he became an alcoholic. He married my mother—a woman he simultaneously adored and feared—in the late 1950s. He adored my mother's doting nature, her adulation, and her attention. But his own mother, the first woman in his life, had taught my father not to trust. He knew the pain of emotional abandonment, and he feared the same fate would befall him if he were vulnerable. Long ago, he protected his emotions behind a wall so thick that even my mother's invariable coaxing could not earn his trust.

My parents' initial months of marital bliss and lustful passion resulted in the birth of my sister. I arrived fourteen months later, and my younger sister—after a slight reprieve for my mother—arrived five years after that. The demands of early motherhood were overwhelming, so my father's newly found source of adulation and sexual fulfillment would soon be denied him. Once again my father felt betrayed by a woman on whom he depended for the self-esteem that he could not supply for himself.

The betrayal and anger my father felt were based in the unconscious, unresolved wounds that had simmered for decades—and which he had learned from his own mother. When my father's wounds were rubbed, his rage descended on me and my sisters—without mercy, justice, or decency, and certainly without self-knowledge. He could not feel his shame.

My father's crimes were, in part, the result of him withdrawing from his shameful acts behind a wall of survivor-mentality fortitude, which wove throughout our entire family system. That fortitude told him that his rage was necessary for survival, and that introspection would reduce him to the needy child he nevertheless remained all his life. Rage and silence—these were his survival tools, and he bequeathed to my sisters and me an energy that seeped deep into our lifeblood, teaching us to fend for ourselves but leaving us in terror of intimacy.

My father's anger at what his childhood had branded into his soul was acted out each and every night. The smell of alcohol and the blank look in his eyes taught me to hide with my sisters and pray for a reprieve. But each night he came, leaving the bed he shared with my mother to take one of us as his prisoner. The squeaks of the door, the thin sliver of light, and the rustling of covers were all part of the ritual. I lay rigid, covers held tight, shallow breaths, closed eyes, like a scared animal burrowing, hoping to evade the advancing predator. I pretended not to see, nor to hear.

When it was my sister he raped, I would creep along the hallway to keep vigil over her suffering, knowing rescue was beyond my grasp. Watching the second hand sweep over the miniscule dots on the oversized face of the wall clock, I pretended that each brush of the hand erased the filth that unfolded below. I sat, clenched jaw, tight stomach, sweaty palms, counting the specks in the linoleum, making up figures in the wallpaper, hating him and fearing him and the acts that were beyond the comprehension of my five-year-old mind.

When it was me he summoned, I learned how to leave my mind and body behind in the warmth of my bed. I delivered him only a shell, a lifeless puppet, one he would use and then discard like garbage. I heard only the rush in my head, felt only the sweat on my skin, saw only stars dancing in front of my eyes, and smelled the stench of his release.

For years this was our fate: terror and violation, night after night. Like my ancestors, I learned to survive, to skew reality, making it all seem normal. I lived a life of duplicity: the split world of God-fearing, churchgoing, white picket fence by day; terror by night. I learned that if we didn't talk about it, didn't think about it, didn't feel it, it didn't exist. That is what trauma does.

I suppressed the memories, but the toxic energy simmers. It simmers just under the surface, seeping out like a slow oil leak until the blackness invades and contaminates all aspects of our lives. My contamination was self-hatred because I couldn't hate the parents on whom, in my child's mind, my life depended. I needed them to protect me, so I figured that there must be something wrong with me that was causing this hurt. It must be my worthlessness, my disgusting self that they were drawn to hurt. If I were prettier, kinder, quieter, smarter, if I were anything other than me, then they would love me, cherish me, and create safety. But no, I am none of those things, and so they hurt me.

This is what happens to abuse survivors. We distort our realities because we cannot live with the esteem-destroying fact that someone who is supposed to protect us is hurting us; someone who is supposed to love and nurture us is violating us. We are compelled, if we are not to drown in a sense of being unfit to live, to distort reality in order to gain the solace of fitting into the family system, no matter how sick it is. For in the mind of a child, to be abandoned by mother and father is death. Adapting our thoughts and behaviors to make abuse tolerable and to ward off the deadly fear of abandonment molds our character. This is what Swiss psychoanalyst Alice Miller sardonically calls "The Drama of the Gifted Child":

When I used the word gifted in the title, I had in mind neither children who receive high grades in school nor children talented in a special way. I simply meant all of us who have survived an abusive childhood thanks to an ability to adapt even to unspeakable cruelty by becoming numb.... Without this gift offered us by nature, we would not have survived.

Adaptations can take many forms. At a very young age, I learned to become hypervigilant of my environment. I was supersensitive to others' moods, body language, and innuendos in order to avoid imagined abuse. If my father entered the house and slammed the door, I would be hypersensitive to his mood. Would he become enraged? Had he been drinking? I could never trust him, so I watched him and everyone else, scouting out their moods.

I also learned that to be emotionally vulnerable was not safe, so I erected walls around my emotions. I used walls of anger, silence, grandiosity, or seduction. Trust was an invitation to betrayal. I would watch and then decide how to respond in order to get what I wanted. I could never ask directly for what I wanted or needed because I had learned that I would not get it, so I learned to manipulate. If my father was in a good mood, I was seductive. If he was angry,

I became silent, angry, or withholding. If I didn't want to hear what he had to say, I used a continuous stream of words to block him. I did this with everyone because I was terrified of being found out for the worthless person my parents had shamed me into believing I was.

This shame was not my own. I was not born with it. I did not earn it. It came from my parents and from their shameful behavior, which, when dumped on me, became part of who I thought I was. I carried it around for them, for certainly they did not have the capacity to recognize their own shamelessness. Carried shame is the instigator of trauma, whereby each reminder of our shame drives us back to the infant ego state in which we first felt our parents' shame. It freezes us in time. It arrests our development.

I come from a lineage filled with trauma and its subsequent, shame-based wounding: self-loathing individuals, all attempting to hide their pain. Each generation passed on the message to the next. My grandmother attempted to control with rages; my grandfather drank and withdrew. Like me, my father watched his parents and imagined that they treated him this way because he was "bad." And so, when he began to parent, he did what he had learned, and passed that same message on to his children.

Once carried shame is absorbed, it is stored in our unconscious and in the cells of our bodies. This poison incubates and leaches out to fuel our dysfunctional adaptations to abuse. We might not remember our abuse for years until it is triggered into memory. The event is cataclysmic.

It was right before my 30th birthday. I was having a talk with my younger sister. She told me she had been doing some personal psychological work and remembered that she had been sexually abused. Up until that point, I had no memories of incest, and I was surprised by my reaction. Instead of denying or dismissing her reality, I felt a visceral shot of affirming energy throughout my mind and body. It was in that moment that I knew the truth.

My abuse had been stored in the cells of my body and, when unlocked, it sent out a surge of released energy. Often, in the course of my life since my initial revelation, this energy bubbles more subtly. For instance, when I began writing this chapter, I thought that I was feeling well and, intellectually, I felt secure dealing with the material. But, about an hour into the work, I got a severe headache and nausea, and I had to lie down. Today I know the signs, and I take action to allow the energy to be released. I am able to take the measures necessary to allow this process to occur, but that was not always the case.

My family had poisonously gifted me with the tools to block emotional pain, like a prizefighter blocking a right cross. Initially, I used walls, dissociation, and distorted reality. As the years wore on, I needed ever more distorted adaptations in order to dodge and avoid the truth.

I began this journey at a very young age. History's slave, I followed the model of prior generations of my dysfunctional family. My behavioral repertoire of obsessive-compulsive or addictive behaviors began to multiply. The behavior of my parents that I modeled most persistently was intensity. I stayed busy—very busy. Like my parents, I conditioned myself to be in perpetual motion, using whatever means I could find to distract myself from my feelings. If someone or something blocked my ability to stay distracted (for instance, if my mother was too busy to take me to the park, or my neighborhood friends were unable to play), there was hell to pay. I would relentlessly and intrusively coax, nag, harass, hound, or manipulate until I got what I wanted.

Day after day, I feverishly concocted means to run from my feelings. I lived in hyperarousal. As I grew older, my calendar was full: schooling, work, meetings, appointments. But still it was not enough. I needed more, always more, to suppress my immense well of pain.

At the onset of puberty, I began starving myself. As my body began to develop, I became terrified that it would draw further attention from my lecherous father. If I stopped eating, I could stay small, evading further perpetration. Controlling my natural development became an obsession. When I received my first training bra, I wore it twenty-four hours a day, keeping my breasts bound in hopes of restraining further growth.

I entered college immature, frightened, and badly prepared academically. For many students, college was a paradisiacal new frontier. Many got their education in the local taverns, pool halls, and twin beds of their dorm rooms. I, too, found most of this teenage hedonism fun, but the prospect of sex terrified me.

Instinctively, I was living in reaction to my abuse, which I had yet to consciously remember. The abuse had taught me that if I "gave in" sexually, I would lose control. Without control, I would be vulnerable. Traumatized as I was, vulnerability would take me back to the soul-destroying terror of incest. I needed protection and, for protection, I chose to stuff myself with food. I went on a compulsive binge diet of doughnuts, pizza, cookies, chips, and beer. I put on 30 pounds the first semester. A wall of fat shielded me from sexual advances.

"Virtue" became another compulsion-obsession. Staying "pure" became my creed. I snubbed the "loose" girls and had little empathy when abortions were needed. I was a virgin and proud of it. I grew grandiose. I'd watched them fall, one after the other, giving in to instincts of the body—the one thing I was determined to control. I saw myself as strong, and them as weak.

My grandiose purity protected me until I fell "in love." As his sexual demands grew more urgent, so did my fears of rejection—if I continued to hold out. Keeping him became much more vital than my virtue. A storehouse of repressed sexual energy was unleashed. My new creed was that sex equaled love. And that's the way it was in the beginning.

When we moved in together, the euphoria ceased and the lies began. I started noticing little things, like his coming home later and later, his unavailability on the weekends, and the smell of perfume after his night out "with the boys." Soon my true love was gone, lost to another, and I was left with what I knew best—betrayal. I wanted to die, wanted to scream, wanted to obliterate him. But instead, I implemented the tools I had inherited from my family: I numbed and blocked my pain. Within a month, I had lost 30 pounds, begun drinking, and found a new man. I was entering the full cycle of obsession and addiction.

I followed this destructive, insane path into a loveless marriage with a drug addict. I filed for divorce. Shortly after came that fateful phone call from my sister, revealing the secret life in the basement with our father. With the truth of my incest history stimulated by her memories, I was overwhelmed by emotions I could not process sanely. I became overwhelmed by out-of-control anger.

Sex became my weapon. I had, in the past, tried shutting down sexually in order to feel in control. I had also tried to find love through sex. Both had proved ineffective. But now I was going to right the wrong. I was going to take back my power. I was going to purge my rage. *I was going to undo the perpetrations by becoming the perpetrator.* No longer was sex about love. Sex was about revenge.

My sexual abuse at the hands of my father had commingled sex with fear, shame, and rage; it charged everything with intensity. The amalgam created in this emotional blast furnace was *sexualized anger.* It lies deep within us, and, once tapped and released, it obliterates its victims. I became a warrior, a skilled executioner, and my murder weapon was sex.

Night after night I sought my prey, using sex as a weapon. I would kill before being killed, but each time I did, I died a little more. My conquests would have to pay for the sins of my father.

Sex became my greatest need. I was in an obsessive trance, out of control, and spiraling toward emotional suicide. I was a junkie looking for my next fix, my next high. I looked for men in grocery stores, in restaurants, through friends, at clubs. But with every high came the descent, the morning after, the shame, the worthlessness, the self-loathing, the betrayal. I had done it to myself. Although my acting-out behaviors were different from his, in the end, I had become *my father.*

The vicious cycle continued. I thought of suicide, a way out. I lay in a pool of tears. I rocked as the tumultuous emotions erupted. I rocked in the fetal position, praying for the redemption of my grief. It is my pain that has driven me to the edge, and now it is that same pain that can lead me to the truth. I know I must stop the cycle that will enslave me in my family's history.

I now know I need help, and so I reach for the phone before I lose my courage. Dialing the treatment center's number, I hear a soft-spoken, kindhearted man answer; perhaps he is a lifeline to my salvation. I listen as he explains their program and answers my questions. My quivering hand takes notes. "Sex addiction," I write. The words stare back at me. I read them over and over, and I know that my life will never be the same.

THREE

Will these people get help? Even if I cannot answer that question, one thing I now know. It fills me with hope and direction. It is more powerful than my fears and my doubts. I know that it is going to be my life's work to understand the engines of sexual dysfunction, to do my best to help the victims who have become the perpetrators of their own pain and of the pain of others.

It is suffering that consumes this room. I see it, taste it, and breathe it. I have come to recognize the common humanity I share with these abused people. I have been just like them, and I feel privileged—even blessed—that I will be able to listen to their stories, not as a superior, "better than" moralist, but as a comrade who has been shown the path of recovery and who found the willingness to walk down it. I will do my part to reveal that path to them as it is revealed to me.

When I finish my presentation, I pack my box of papers and drive back down the foggy hill. I know that this is the beginning of my new life.

Chapter 2

HOLDING THE SHAME

notice an unusual gray outside, as I adjust the blinds in my office—but then, it *is* the monsoon season. It is a time of year I particularly love—for several reasons. There is first the unprecedented smell stirred when the large droplets of rain hit the dust-laden land, a sweet and earthy richness that pervades the senses. The smell immediately connects me back to the earth.

These monsoons are fast and furious storms that sweep through the desert, volatile in nature and often unpredictable in their destruction. The storms contain microbursts, which are rain combined with winds of up to 60 miles per hour; they can knock down power lines, rip off roofs, and produce sheets of rains so torrential that it is impossible to see farther than your outstretched hand. These bursts usually last only a few minutes, and then the sky clears and returns to its proverbial blue, sunny glow.

Often you can see these storms coming from miles away. The sky turns purple and crimson, and the gray sheets of rain pound the earth below. As I finish adjusting the blinds, I see no dramatic atmospheric displays, so I continue to ready the office for my first client of the day.

When Milton arrives, he seems nervous and untrusting. His eyes dart around the room, his face a blank.

"Have a seat," I say invitingly. Milton responds without saying a word. His eyes are now fierce and piercing. He appears to be in a hypervigilant state, his breath shallow, his body rigid. I understand how frightened, pained, and confused Milton must feel. It is the kind of discomfort that I, a recovering sex addict, lived with on my first visit to a therapist. It continued for many years.

I am sensitive to Milton's painful predicament, but I am equally sensitive to the great gift that may be in store for me. As I begin my relationship with Milton, I know that if we do our work, he will come to trust me enough to hold his pain and shame and suffering.

He will place his dark-side secrets into my hands, until he has developed enough strength and understanding to own them for himself. He knows I will hold them respectfully. This "holding of the shame" is key to all my clients' recovery—and is the abiding gift of my profession. That I can contain such pain safely beyond my boundaries is self-affirming evidence of my own recovery.

"Tell me what brings you into treatment," I ask Milton, noticing how his color has faded to match the gray, billowing clouds outside. Nervously adjusting his position, he responds, "I saw your ad in the weekly 'newspaper.'" (My advertisement runs in a local sex-themed newsletter and offers help to those struggling with compulsive sexual behavior.) This means that Milton has probably not had prior treatment or ever discussed his secret behavior with anyone outside his own circle of addicts.

"Oh, I see," I say in a warm tone. "So what made you call me?"

"I am sick of my life," he says, his body slightly softening.

"Um hmm," I respond, nodding my head. "I am glad you had the courage to call."

A clap of thunder booms through the office as if to affirm his difficult decision. Milton jumps, startled by the loud noise.

Through a slow and arduous interview, Milton explains his behavior, his use of prostitutes, and his masturbation to pornography. At the end of our first meeting, Milton looks drained.

"How are you feeling?" I ask.

"Well, this was different," he says with a slight chuckle.

"How so?" I prompt.

"Well, I have never told anybody this stuff before."

"And how does that feel?"

"I guess good, but . . ." he says, trailing off.

"But, what?" I ask.

"Well, how did I ever get this way? I must be some kind of sicko pervert to do this stuff."

The rain has now begun to pummel the windows as the wind roars, fiercely scraping the branches of the ironwood tree against the stucco wall. I can't help but wonder whether this torrential storm reflects how Milton feels. Is he feeling the enormous release of a lifetime of secrets and shame? A fierce cleansing, like the torrents of rain that are carving away at the exposed and barren earth? If so, he does not say. He seems to merely accept my validation that he is not a "sicko," but is, rather, a person who learned unhealthy and destructive ways to express his sexuality.

As we begin our work together, Milton soon discovers that, like a lot of other sex addicts, his shame is embedded in his childhood trauma. Like all children, Milton needed nurturing and love, a consistent mirroring from his parents to reinforce his sense of well-being and safety. Unfortunately, Milton's mother was incapable of giving this nurturing love to her son because she was mentally ill.

Milton lived in a whirlwind of unpredictable behavior and emotions. When his mother was in a stable mood, she doted on his every whim. However, when she became psychotic or lost touch with reality, Milton was frightened and bewildered. Milton walked on eggshells and learned to prepare himself for the emotional storm that inevitably erupted each day. This left Milton hypervigilant to his environment. He learned to watch for the nuances in his mother's moods, changes in her physical gestures, a distant look in her eyes, a quick, jerky movement of her arms; Milton knew to brace himself. Her erratic behavior took many forms, but the most difficult for Milton occurred when she stripped off her clothes and ran stark naked around the house and yard, singing, dancing, and talking incessantly.

Milton was an only child; his father was a truck driver who would be absent for extended periods. This left Milton to fend for himself. He blamed himself for his mother's mood swings and erratic behavior, and believed that he triggered her outbursts.

Seeing his mother naked was at first a shock, but this erratic behavior soon became the norm. As Milton grew older and began to develop sexually, his mother's behavior became a profound influence in the imprinting of his sexual identity. His mother's behavior left Milton feeling anger, fear, danger, arousal, and intensity—a strange and powerful menagerie of emotions that became embedded in his sexual expression.

Milton's first masturbatory fantasies were of his mother, and, when he began to see prostitutes, he had them act out his mother's erratic behaviors. Milton learned to do what all sex addicts do, which is to repeat what they have learned from their childhood wounds.

My work with Milton, as with all my clients, becomes a collaboration. It is through our collaborative effort that trust, understanding, and respect begin to unfold. He will willingly off-load into my outstretched hands his darkest secrets.

I hope that all of my clients can metaphorically find in me the selflessly respectful, nurturing parent they never had. I hope they will allow me to store their sick behaviors and demeaning beliefs and emotions until they themselves are willing to acknowledge and deal with them. I become the solid ego state against which the wounded ego can collide, yet survive. I mirror for them the respect, understanding, and safety they have never known. The wounded part begins to heal. The therapist becomes the good parent. The client internalizes that identity. The healing takes place within the therapeutic relationship.

One of the most challenging aspects of Milton's treatment comes when he begins to face his dysfunctional attachment to his primary caregiver. From this attachment, Milton developed a deep sense of betrayal. Through the dysfunctional bonding, Milton internalized the wound and ended up feeling that, because he was not worthy of love, the betrayal by his caretakers was his own fault. What ultimately develops from this wounding is an entire psychic life that rests on a bed of shame and resentment.

I like the idea that it is my responsibility as a therapist to hold temporarily for the client the burden of this shame. I respectfully and skillfully urge the client to describe his or her shame and the behavior it has generated. The client hands it off to me for storage until that time in our therapy when I can hand it back to him or her for inspection. At that point, the client has grown able to appreciate that he or she is not endemically evil, but is the victim of abuse.

I am able to hold the shame, the anxious hope, whatever belief system, or whatever emotion the client is feeling, and say to this suffering and trusting person, "You know what? I believe you can work through this, and that you can and will become even more than you now believe is possible. And I will hold all the shame or other emotion for you while we are doing this work together."

In our subsequent meetings, I want Milton to confess and describe all of his sexual behaviors in detail. I have a checklist of about forty types of behaviors, each of which can cause arousal (including sex with animals, with a minor, urination, asphyxiation, voyeurism, exhibitionism, sadomasochism, cross-dressing, and so on).

I ask Milton to tell me whether he has participated in any of the aberrant activities in the checklist. Going through the checklist often facilities the first trusting moments in my relationship with a client. When he or she realizes in our first or second meeting that I am comfortable discussing these activities, the client realizes that I cannot be shocked. He or she senses that I have enough experience to know that whatever behavior the person has engaged in, I am there to understand, not to judge. This was best described by a veteran client who said, "The first time I trusted you was when you pulled out that checklist of sexual behaviors, because if you could ask those questions and not seem to freak out, I figured you could handle my problems."

The goal of early treatment is to help clients trust that I respect them in their full humanity, even the darkest parts. I want them to understand that I can deal with their demons and find the healthy soul trapped within. This is the beginning of the holding of the shame.

"So, Milton," I begin, "I will read this list, and you tell me whether you have participated in any of these behaviors."

Milton's eyes once again dart around the room as his body stiffens. I surmise that Milton's discomfort has just shifted into overdrive.

"Just let me know whether you have ever done any of these. And if you have and would like to explain anything," I attempt to say in a reassuring tone, "go right ahead."

There is no visible shift in Milton's expression or posture.

It is only through much discussion and "excavation" that Milton is able to admit to other acting-out behaviors not previously disclosed, including multiple affairs and exposing himself.

"Withholding information is very common in early treatment," I say to Milton. "It is shame that keeps us from telling the truth," I continue. "Nobody wants to talk about these behaviors, but by taking this step, you come that much closer to healing."

Milton seems less than reassured by my comments as he sits, staring blankly into space. He looks as though he's had the wind kicked out of him and may be on the verge of hyperventilating. Even though this early work is painstakingly tough for the client, I find it fascinating.

The first time I meet a new client, I am looking at a history about to be told, a life about to be given form. At first the story of this life will be a complex puzzle, which later will fit together into a coherent clinical picture. My client, usually my only source of information, lives in delusion and denial. I had better be very attentive and very patient.

I gather information on a lot of different levels. First of all, I look at what is happening to my clients' bodies: how they are sitting, the tone of voice they are using. Are they angry, are they shy, are they withholding, are they shamed, are they animated or enervated? I want to find out how they hold their wounding and all the shame associated with that. What postures, both emotional and physical, have they molded into their "suit of armor" to protect against the attacks of their shaming?

When I was a primary therapist at The Meadows (a multidisorder inpatient facility specializing in treatment of a broad range of addictions), I would never look at any paperwork about a client until I had met with the individual personally. I wanted to understand what she was like, to experience the texture of what she had to say, and to reflect on her most repeated themes. Only then would I read all the clinical and written material that had been gathered about her and her problems.

Like most clients, Milton is lost in confusion about what lies behind his addictive behaviors. The next task in treatment, therefore, is to help Milton understand his behavior—to unravel the reasons he engages in these specific sexual acts, and determine how these patterns and beliefs came to be. I am "normalizing" Milton's behavior for him, not condoning it. He will come to understand that the way he was abused created traumatic templates for him, which he was powerless to change.

As I listen to Milton's story, I look for patterns in his trauma. This historical excavation must unveil the connections between his wounding and his acting-out behaviors. As we explore the layers of traumatic events in Milton's life, I want to be able to make those connections—even more importantly, I want Milton to begin to connect the dots.

As this begins to happen, Milton happily reports, "I feel less and less like a perverted sicko."

It is a simple equation: As the awareness and understanding become more clear, the shame automatically begins to reduce.

I am particularly keen about victimization. Do patients see themselves as victims? How did they become victims in their own minds? Who taught them to be victims? What are they gaining from being victims? How do they use the power of victimhood to manipulate others?

And so I notice that, when Milton explains his childhood and history of significant relationships, he repeatedly uses the phrase, "She [or he or they] made me feel this way. . . ."

"When I was a kid," he begins, "my mother was always telling me what to do, and that made me feel like I was a bad kid. When my father would scream at me and call me stupid in front of my friends, that made me feel mortified. In high school, my girlfriend had this really loud laugh, and it made me feel embarrassed. My dog took a crap on my aunt's carpeting when we were visiting, and it made me feel like crawling in a hole. My wife is so demanding, it makes me feel inadequate." On and on the list goes.

This theme, which was indicated and perpetuated by Milton's parents' inability to be supportive, taught him to feel like a victim. As children, we are all victims when exposed to any type of abuse, because we are unable to defend or protect ourselves from it.

Abuse can take many forms and be experienced in many ways. Most abuse is not intentional. It usually is an unconscious pattern or repetition of what the caregiver learned from his or her own childhood. The definition of abuse I use comes from Pia Mellody's work, and is defined in her book *The Intimacy Factor* as "anything less than nurturing." When abuse is defined in this manner, it can encompass a large spectrum of behaviors and situations.

When I train therapists and share that definition, I can sense a definite shift in the room. A collective gasp erupts as the audience members take inventory of their own parenting skills, and realize that they have at times been less-than-nurturing parents.

I will then stop, acknowledge what is happening, and remind the audience that, within the human condition, traumatic events both large and small are inevitable. This does not condone abusive behavior, but it acknowledges the many levels of its existence. As therapists, it is our job to help our clients first become aware of abusive patterns or events—not in an effort to blame, but to understand and ultimately to resolve the original wounding.

There are two ways abuse can manifest; the first is overt abuse. Overt abuse is usually aggressive behavior that is measurable, such as bruises, a raised voice, a verbal attack, or an insult. The second is covert abuse. Covert abuse is passive, often unconscious, and not seen as abusive (such as withholding love, giving a stern or threatening look, failing to protect a child, or minimizing his or her realities). One can be abused covertly and/or overtly and, no matter how the abuse is perpetrated, it always leaves victims feeling shame and pain on some level.

Clients often have normalized abusive behavior or, even worse, blame themselves for the abuse. "If I hadn't been drunk, I wouldn't have been raped." "Putting each other down is just what my family does." When I point out that these are examples of abuse, I am often met with denial, defensiveness, or confusion.

Because of these common reactions, it is important to grasp the scope of abuse and to become aware of how abuse may have affected or influenced one's life. Below is an outline of the types of abuse, with examples of specific behaviors in each category.

I. Physical Abuse (any forced or violent physical action)

- Hitting
- Punching
- Scratching
- Spitting
- Pushing
- Burning
- Choking
- Poking
- Unsolicited touching or tickling
- Restraining
- Pulling hair
- Slapping

II. Emotional or Verbal Abuse (putting down, threatening, and saying cruel or untrue things about another person)

- Cursing, swearing, screaming
- Harassing or interrogating
- Insulting, name-calling, shaming, ridiculing
- Threatening to harm; beat up; sabotage; hurt; maim or kill pets, children, or family members
- Controlling others (e.g., through money or power)
- Criticizing
- Forcing others to engage in degrading acts
- Making accusations
- Blaming
- Intimidating
- Punching, throwing, destroying property
- Going through others' property or possessions
- Stealing
- Threatening to kill oneself as a form of manipulation
- Sexualizing others
- Driving recklessly
- Stalking
- Not letting others sleep or eat
- Making facial expressions or physical gestures that indicate judgment, rejection, ridicule (e.g., smirking, covering the ears as if unwilling to listen, walking out of the room while someone is sharing, rolling the eyes, shaking the head, moving the hands in a manner indicating that the other is wrong or inadequate)

III. Sexual Abuse (any nonconsensual sexual act, behavior, or gesture)

- Not respecting "no"
- Making sexual remarks, jokes, innuendos, suggestions, insults
- Taking advantage of situations and exploiting others' intoxication or incapacitation
- Demanding or manipulating unwanted sexual acts (e.g., anal penetration, physical restriction, choking, golden showers, oral sex, sadomasochistic acts, role-playing)
- Having unprotected sex while knowingly having a sexually transmittable disease
- Giving sexual criticism
- Engaging in inappropriate touching (e.g., touching in public, grabbing, pinching the breast or groin)
- Blackmailing or manipulating the vulnerable (i.e., the much younger and/or sexually inexperienced, the disabled, the mentally or emotionally challenged)
- Taking advantage of a power differential (e.g., the case of a boss, clergy member, lawyer, judge, law enforcement officer, landlord, teacher, coach)

IV. Neglect (failing to provide the essential necessities for a child, including the following)

- Nurturance
- Clothing
- Medical care

- Dental care
- Security
- Protection
- Hygiene
- Education
- Supervision
- Shelter
- Attention to physical, emotional, intellectual needs

This outline does not include every possible abusive behavior, but it does provide an overview of abuse. This awareness is vital to healing, because it is through creating awareness and resolution that we will act as sexually mature people in healthy manners.

Being mature means taking responsibility for our actions and setting limits or boundaries with others. When we are able to act in a mature way, we will create the safety, respect, and sense of well-being we deserve.

This is what happened to Milton as he began to understand his abuse. He learned that he felt disempowered as a child because of the continual fear, guilt, and shaming he received, particularly from his mother. As he grew up, he was unable to resolve these shameful messages, and so he continued to react as he always had—as a victim. From this stance, Milton felt vulnerable and powerless. To counter these unbearable feelings—and fostered by his feelings of anger—he moved to the role of perpetrator. "I am not good enough; I'll masturbate." "My wife doesn't appreciate me; I'll have an affair." "My boss is an asshole; I'll pick up a prostitute."

The wreckage of such abuse leaves all sex addicts with a sense of betrayal so severe that they lose the ability to trust. They are convinced that if they are seen or really known, they will be despised. But when I can establish a bond of trust, we can have a respectful attachment—a place at which the healing can begin.

It can take more than a year for clients to begin building a strong connection and to trust me with their darkest secrets. This was true for Milton. Although we had done a lot of healing the previous year, it was not until the ominous clouds converged in the sky overhead and the winds began to howl that he revealed his most painful secret: Milton's mother had molested him while in her psychotic breaks. She had touched his genitals as she danced naked in front of him, and she had forced him to touch her breast. After the touching became a familiar ritual, Milton began touching his mother without prompting.

When Milton's mother reentered reality, she remembered nothing; Milton remembered it all. Like most survivors of sexual abuse, Milton felt fear, confusion, shame, and excitement. Too afraid to tell anyone, he learned what was perhaps his most powerful coping skill. He learned to live a double life—a life of secrets and lies, where shame festers, multiplies, and spreads like a deadly cancer.

As the stress of his split world intensified, Milton's anxiety grew more and more intolerable until he did the unthinkable. While babysitting the neighbors' children, he crept into the five-year-old's room while she slept and molested her. He did what had been done to him. When he moved from victim to perpetrator, Milton felt temporary emotional relief. For those few moments, he felt in control. He felt powerful. He felt relief.

When Milton had finished his disclosure, he was completely demoralized. But if he had been unable to fully divulge his secret life, his self-loathing would have poisoned him, and kept him from enough self-value to think he was worthy of recovery. By putting those pieces together and revealing the truth of his trauma history, Milton could finally understand and release the shame wound that made him the creature of his compulsions. His act of trust in me is at the center of his healing, because once he managed to establish that bond, his deepest healing process could begin.

As Milton sits across from me, the rains are once again pummeling the windows, the skies are rumbling, and the old ironwood tree rattles against the stucco wall. It is now that Milton can fully tell his story; he's finally able to explain the shame that was born of his traumatic wounding. He has gained the insight that led to the discovery of his truth. And this is when, automatically, he begins to cut loose from the bondage of shame.

"I finally feel free," he explains. "That secret has dragged down my heart for so long," he says with a slight smile.

Again his look is distant, and his shoulders are slumped—except this time, the distant look and slumped shoulders are not from carrying his burdensome shame. Rather, they are from his road-weary travels, a journey that has allowed him to return to a feeling of well-being.

And so, as always at the end of a fierce storm, the rain begins to cease, the winds settle into quiet slumber, and Milton gently sighs, whispering, "I finally feel free. I'm finally free." As he says this, it is as if, in simultaneous union, the proverbial blue, sunny sky breaks through, allowing a sliver of light to filter through the blinds. Perhaps this is a light of hope, a light of promise, or simply the light after a good storm that allows us to feel cleansed, renewed, and restored.

Chapter 3

TRAUMA AND DISTORTION

Undoing the Abuse

At the heart of every sexually dysfunctional person who acts out is the desire to undo the abuse suffered in childhood at the hands of more powerful, controlling abusers. The difference is that, as children, sexually dysfunctional persons suffered the punishment; as adults, they dish it out. As children, they had no power or control; as adults, they take power and control. Sexual compulsive behavior is not about sex; it is about power and control.

This desire to undo the abuse is the modus operandi behind almost all sexual deviance. In my therapy, if I can help a patient understand his acting-out behaviors as attempts to "undo the abuse," he has come a long way toward the path of recovery.

In sexual addiction, we learn to continually betray ourselves. Our childhood wounding provides our source of betrayal. We learn betrayal because our parents betrayed us. Their jobs as parents were to keep us safe, to nurture us, and to help us thrive. Instead they taught us, either through covert or overt abuse or abandonment, that we did not deserve to be loved. We did not deserve to feel safe. Perhaps we did not deserve even to take up space on this planet.

When people get into healing trauma and early recovery work, they do not yet know how to stop betraying themselves. They allow themselves to do things outside their value system, which continually eats away at their self-worth and perpetuates the conviction that "I am wrong. I am bad. I am unworthy. I am not deserving."

By acting against our value systems, by allowing ourselves to be led back to the world of our original wounding where we learned that we were worthless and inadequate, we trap ourselves in the cycles of sexual addiction. Our trauma templates are our maps back to the place of our original wounding.

Trauma and Repetition

It is Christmas Eve in rural Missouri. A dusting of snow covers the frozen ground, lights twinkle from the warm farmhouses, and smoke drifts from the chimneys as if it were beckoning Santa and his eight reindeer to the eager children below. It has not been an easy year for Joe and his family; then again, in Joe's eight short years, ease has been a sparse commodity. His parents are hard-working, God-fearing folks who live by the land, with Mother Earth in control of their fate. This life, carved more from brawn than brains, is the only life Joe has known.

He has toughened to meet the requirements of this life and finds rewards in the sweet and simple offerings of his daily routines: the soft and gentle nuzzle from his mare, the dawn revealing a rainbow of light, the richly-plowed fields lined neatly across the land, the picking of green apples accompanied by visions of freshly baked pies.

Joe also has learned from life's hardships: the monotonous shoveling, raking, mowing, tilling, hauling, feeding, and plowing. He has lived with the scorching heat of summer, the brutal snowstorms of winter, and the rain and mud of fall and spring. Then there are the fiscal hardships, such as waiting to replace the soles on his boots until the harvested grain has been sold. His clothes, twelve years old, are now faded and torn; the scars on his brother's hand-me-downs show the rough-and-tumble life of two small farm hands. Asking for more is forbidden, but wishing for it is Joe's favorite pastime.

Joe still believes in the magic of Christmas and the hope that Santa will bring him the fanciful bounty he imagines. The white sheet under the Christmas tree they chopped down lies barren, but tomorrow it will overflow with packages, and the thought leaves Joe dizzy with delight.

Each night before he falls asleep, Joe says his prayers, the same prayers he's said his entire life. Only in the past few months has Joe added this request: "And please, God, have Santa bring a new toolbox."

As in many children's fantasies, Joe wants to feel special; he wants to feel as if he can ask for and receive the love and nurturing he needs. It is the birthright of all children to be cared for, both emotionally and physically. However, not all caregivers are able to meet their children's needs.

In trying to understand the roots of my patients' illnesses, the childhood needs that have become most relevant are the needs to be physically and emotionally cared for. When the child's primary caregivers properly provide that care, the child safely and lovingly bonds with his parents. In so doing, he is given a model of the world in which he has peaceful expectations of safety and happiness. He develops self-esteem and feels he is worthwhile. Such people do not become my clients.

However, when one of the child's needs is rejected, he concludes that his caregivers do not think him worthy of love. He does not blame them; he blames himself. Even if his father beats him, he blames no one more than himself.

The child suffers a traumatic blow to his self-esteem. If the child were not helpless at this stage of his life, he would express his anger or indeed his rage. Instead he feels shame and a form of trauma that will enable him to dismiss the reality of what he has experienced.

Joe lies still in his bed, listening intently for the sound of prancing hooves. But all he hears is the predictable train whistle that passes each morning at three, the ticking of the grandfather clock in the entryway, and the breathing of his brother sleeping in the bunk above. Joe hears no clanking or clatter from the rooftop.

Joe's prayers for his shiny new toolbox are born out of his Saturday and Sunday afternoons (Sunday mornings are reserved for church services), which are spent fixing the machinery that runs the farm. Often his grandfather and uncle come down to lend a hand. Joe loves the large and spacious garage. He finds comfort in the familiar, greasy oil stains on the flattened cardboard boxes strategically placed under the cars to catch the inevitable leaks.

And he loves when the afternoon light reflects off the lids of jars meticulously nailed to the wooden beams. Lined up in military precision, the jars hold a fascinating variety of nails and other items. But the most prized possessions of all are the worn, red metal toolboxes sitting atop their tall stands. Smeared with greasy fingerprints and draped with filthy work towels, each box is a treasure chest to Joe.

He has spent many hours sitting on the propane tanks, watching intently as his father and brothers twist, pull, crank, and prod various types of machinery. Joe does not dare join the others because the few times he did, unable to contain his curiosity, his father's hickory switch strategically slapped his backside.

Having his own toolbox is Joe's passport to this much coveted world—a world important not because of the mysteries it holds, but because of the emotional connection it promises.

When a child's instinctual needs for love, physical care, and coaching go unmet, the memory of that deprivation becomes imprinted in his psyche. Because the child believes it is because of his own inadequacy that his needs are not being fulfilled, his personality and his life come to be shame based. All trauma gets its power from this original shaming.

As the morning light filters in and the first rooster's crow is heard, Joe flies out of bed and races into the living room. The magic has happened once more. Santa has arrived and, for this moment in time, all is right with the world. Seeing the sparkling ribbons and bows so neatly tied, Joe can hardly stand his excitement. Before the others rouse from their slumber, Joe plops himself among the packages, shaking each one and reading each name tag for possible clues. He assesses the packages—one heavy, one light, one long, one short. Nothing seems to fit until . . . he spies a large package in the back, camouflaged by a drooping tree branch. It's heavy, it has his name on it, and, when he shakes it, it rattles; could this be his coveted toolbox? A few more shakes, and he is sure this is his prized possession.

Joe has to wait for what seems an eternity until the family huddles around the tree to begin to open the presents. Joe dives for his package, furiously rips off the bow, tears off the paper, and frantically opens the box. Because of his frenzied gestures, all the others have been distracted and are now fixated on Joe. His face is frozen, his eyes dilated, and his breath heavy as he looks and sees the contents of his box: bricks. Joe feels dizzy; the room is spinning so fast he can hardly hear the hearty laughter of his family. "We got ya', didn't we, Joey?" he faintly hears his father say. He fights back the tears until the lump in his throat feels as though it could choke him.

Shame is the predominating feeling, and it fuels the adaptations that protect the child from actually experiencing it. No matter what disguise he adopts in order to fit into the family system, at the bottom, his emotions will rest on a bed of shame.

What develops is a walled-off, highly defended, frightened person who will trust no one other than himself. This need to handle everything by himself removes him from all cooperative intimacy; it denies him any level of intimacy with self or with others.

For Joe, the emotional scars from Christmas morning lay branded deep in his soul. His father's practical joke, although not intended as such, was emotional abuse. Joe's father was carrying on a longstanding family tradition. When the youngest child was old enough, the parents would deliberately trick him into thinking he was getting his coveted present. The men in Joe's family had perpetrated this psychological hazing on each other for decades. It was not intended to be cruel; Joe's father was only doing what he knew to do, what had been done to him.

Building tough character was the foundation of Joe's family tree. And Joe's father was the architect of Joe's emotional fate—laying mortar and bricks one by one until Joe's feelings were securely sealed away.

In his book *I Don't Want to Talk about It: Overcoming the Secret Legacy of Male Depression*, Terry Real asserts that trauma and the resulting repression of feelings are the foundation for depression. Although this is true for both men and women, men's cultural conditioning teaches them to refine this process to perfection. Terry describes the issue:

"To understand depression in men, we must come to terms with the conditions that create it, the ways in which, in the name of masculinity and often with the best of intentions, we betray and deform our sons."

Depression is often defined as "anger turned inward." And most men and women are angry (mostly unconsciously) about the fact that they had to secure those walls, stuff those feelings, and pretend they didn't hurt. This kind of conditioning is the breeding ground for all addictions.

In my early work with clients, I want them to look behind the walls and under the anger, and to feel the pain. The problem, especially for men, is that such behavior runs counter to their conditioning, and it is terrifying.

Joe now stands six feet tall and has come to me, looking for help. His appearance—a tautly drawn jaw; severe, stern eyes; and a rock-solid stance—is a tribute to years of his father's work. He is a man entombed, isolated from connection—a lonely, empty vessel adrift in an ocean of shame.

As Joe's therapist, I want to build enough trust with him to let him know that I am not there to tear him down or to perpetuate the abuse he suffered. I want him to understand that I am there to help him believe that he has real worth, and that he deserves to feel secure. I want him to feel that he has a right to create an environment for himself in which he not only feels safe, but one in which he is able and ready to begin working on having healthy intimate relationships.

However, Joe's walls of emotional protection are securely embedded. He has become extremely rigid and angry in order to protect his underlying feelings of fear, pain, and shame. When he feels threatened or vulnerable, he falls into a feeling of shame—in Pia Mellody's work, such a feeling is called "the one-down position." He will feel "less than" anyone else in the world.

Despite the fact that Joe is attractive, intelligent, full of humor, and successful in his own farming business, he will once again feel like that child who was devastated by the Christmas prank. He slips back into the feeling that everything is hopeless and that he is helpless. When a person is in such a state, he has a childlike ego. He has been propelled back into that original trauma, reexperiencing it in his mind, body, and emotions.

In order to protect himself from being propelled back into this painful place, he returns to that walled-off position where he feels protected yet totally disempowered and vulnerable.

Perhaps the oddest result of inappropriate parenting occurs when a child is given the false and dangerous notion that he is better and more powerful than others. This "false empowerment" is what Pia Mellody calls "the one-up position," and grandiosity is the predominating feeling. However, from this position of "one-up" grandiosity, the child will not be able to enter into mutually loving relationships; he'll be as lonely and deprived in relationship as if he were "one-down." In either case, the child will not know how to love or be loved, to respect or be respected.

As is often the case for my clients, Joe's wounding has left him feeling both one-down, or disempowered, and alternately, one-up and falsely empowered. He was disempowered, partially by the males in the family, by being denied emotional support and validation. His relationship with his mother Kay was an altogether different story.

Joe's mother's desire to parent was abundant. Having grown up as the eldest in a family of twelve, the dye of her destiny had been cast early. She was not only well skilled in the care and tending of small children, she also adored doing so. Her plans were to have at least the same number of children as her mother had. Because she and Joe's father had known each other from birth and their farms bordered each other, he was well aware of her love of children. Kay's plans to have a large family suited him fine because he believed it meant that he would have more helping hands to run the farm.

As they had planned earlier in the marriage, Joe and his brothers were spaced two years apart. Married at twenty-two, Kay planned to give birth to her last child at the age of forty-six.

Each of Kay's children brought her immense joy. However, Kay—a short, slight woman standing only five-foot-one—had a difficult childbirth with each of her children. She sustained two miscarriages, as well as several medical conditions, that ultimately led to her hysterectomy at the age of thirty. The devastation she felt was profound. She became severely depressed and, although she pushed herself to continue her familial duties, it was an arduous effort. She kept these feelings from her husband so as not to burden him with her problems. She remained "strong," despite feeling as if she could crumble, at any moment, into a million pieces.

To cope with her grief, she poured her energy and attention onto her youngest son. Extremely dependent on her, young Joe became the emotional balm to ease her pain. Joe became the center of her world, the focus of her joy. She lived for him, and his accomplishments and successes became hers. This emotional dependency grew like a cancer, infecting all aspects of their relationship.

Kay became more and more distant from her husband, transferring her needs for emotional intimacy to Joe. She began to confide her problems and concerns to him. In response, he became hypersensitive to his mother's moods, gestures, tones and expressions, as he felt more and more responsible for her happiness.

But there was a problem with Joe's beatification of his mother because Joe felt conflicted in his feelings toward her. He felt special, even privileged, to replace the role of her husband, but he was also very angry with her. Joe's mother expected Joe to fulfill her emotional needs, thus abandoning his own needs and wants. In addition, he felt pressure to be perfect in order to please his mother, to perform in ways that would make her proud—like being elected class president or making the football team. When he received accolades in the local paper, he felt all the emotional credit going to his mother rather than to himself. Joe later became successful in business and in that, too, he felt that he was working for his mother, not for himself.

For Joe's entire childhood, the focus was not really on Joe; it was on pleasing his mother. Pleasing his mother was how Joe learned to feel safe.

So Joe's trauma etched dual realities (each one false) into his self-perception. The first, inherited from his father, told him he was "less than." The second, provided by his mother, told him he was "better than"—better than his brothers, better than his peers, even better than his father. This "one-up, better-than" position ultimately left Joe in extreme emotional isolation. He also experienced extreme fear because if Joe made one mistake, failed to produce or perform, or was less than perfect in his own mind's eye, then Joe would be rejected.

Both the one-down position and the one-up position result from failures of a child's primary caregivers to acknowledge the innate preciousness of their child. One adaptation can be as harmful to the child's sense of inherent worth as the other. The falsely empowered child, who has been as badly treated as the one-down child, may be more difficult to cure, because, in his grandiosity, he is unaware that his false empowerment is a form of abandonment. His parents never taught him how to be relational, but he remains unaware that he is deprived because he feels so grandiose. He will be deaf to the suggestions of his therapists that he, too, is shamed and, at bottom, one-down. In either case, the child has suffered abandonment because his caregivers left him without the crucial ability to develop self-esteem.

When, early in treatment, I told Joe that I thought he was really angry with his mother, he got defensive. In fact, Joe was so put off that he almost terminated treatment.

Unraveling the truth about Joe's relationship with his mother would become a slow and sometimes grief-filled process. But as the process opened him up to the truth, we were gradually able to get to the root of his sexualized anger, manifested in his sexual addiction.

It is a hot summer day as Joe sits slumped in my office. He has been coming regularly to therapy for several months and has applied his lifetime legacy of hard work to this process.

"I love my wife, but . . ." Joe says, trailing off.

"But what?" I ask.

"I just feel so much pressure, like I am not enough."

"What do you mean, not enough?"

"You know, like whatever I do is not enough."

"Explain to me what that looks like."

"Well, last week was Mother's Day, and I got her a spa package. I thought it was a good gift because she is always complaining about how tired she gets taking care of our boys. But when I forgot to pick up the potato salad for the barbecue, she flew off the handle, went nuts, said if it's going to get done right that she had to do it . . . and she had to do everything. Then she turned to me and told me I could take my present back because I really did not mean it."

"How did that feel?"

"Shitty."

"It sounds painful."

"Yeah," he says. "It was."

"What is it like to live with someone who is so angry with you?"

"Painful."

"And so, to ease the pain, you go to prostitutes?"

"Um hmm. . . ."

"And I'm pissed," he says with more force, "because she's always riding my case."

"What would it be like if you were in a relationship that was loving and supportive?"

"I would screw it up," Joe says.

In his marriage, Joe has re-created the same childhood beliefs he experienced toward his mother: "I have to be perfect to be loved. I have to abandon myself to be in relationship." These beliefs created a vicious, lifelong cycle because imperfection is inherent in the human condition. The harder Joe attempted to be perfect, the more he failed. And the more he failed, the more shame he felt. And the more shame he felt, the angrier he became.

As a child, Joe could not get angry with his mother because of his dependence upon her. As an adult, he can. Joe now takes the anger he has repressed and acts it out in his relationship with his wife by hiring prostitutes.

Joe now has clarity about the dynamic related to his anger at his mother. However, Joe, like many recovering sex addicts, feels confused as to why his anger became sexualized. It becomes crucial for all recovering sex addicts to understand the cause and effect of their behaviors because unlocking this mystery becomes the cornerstone of healing.

The answer lies in examining a person's trauma history. No matter how trauma is manifested, whether overtly or covertly, disempowering or falsely empowering, it will create a trauma template, a lens that one looks through that results in delusion. The primal response to trauma is to survive, and so, in adults, the unconscious drive becomes to "undo" or "fix" the original trauma. The initial attempts at undoing or fixing the wounding provide temporary emotional relief, but ultimately the results are profound pain and shame.

Like Joe, many of my clients feel lost, confused, or severely conflicted between their value systems and their acting-out behaviors. On a conscious level, they want a sense of congruence, but it seems out of their grasp. Often they feel the unconscious drive into self-destructive behaviors—like a strong tide washing them out to sea. They feel powerless against its forceful pull. The goal of treatment is to make the unconscious templates conscious. This "connecting of the dots," or etiological understanding, is crucial to all clients' recovery because without it they will remain in a haze of confusion, repetition, and shame.

Joe's relationship with his mother is like that of many heterosexual men I treat. His mother's abuse was not overtly sexual. It was covertly incestuous. Covert sexual abuse occurs when the child becomes the surrogate spouse to the parent. This dynamic creates unconscious bonding and can feel sexually charged, even without any overt behavior or gestures. It is as if the loving energy that is natural and healthy between a husband and wife begins to transfer or spill over onto the child. The nature of this attachment is sexual, and so the child picks up or absorbs this energy, which results in covert sexual abuse.

Joe's emotions, when squeezed through these destructive trauma templates, directed him to seek fulfillment in self-destructive behaviors. The narcotic aim of such behavior was to protect him from reexperiencing the pain and shame of feeling unworthy of love, unsafe, and undeserving. These dysfunctional adaptations may reduce pain, but they ultimately yield the same shame and pain that they temporarily allay. All trauma templates repeat the original wound because they return the trauma victim to the ego-state of the original infliction.

Joe's awareness of his sexual abuse was powerfully exemplified several weeks after we discussed the dynamic.

"You know how we have been talking about my mother and her using me emotionally?" he asked.

"Yes."

"Well, the weirdest thing happened the other day. I was sitting in my truck talking with her. The door of the cab was open, and she tried to sit on my lap."

"Oh, my. What happened next?"

"I pushed her off," he said, gesturing as if he still needed to push her away.

"How did that feel?"

"It was weird, creepy."

"Had you been aware of this kind of behavior before?"

"Not until we started to talk about it."

"Could you connect with how you must have felt as a child?"

"Yeah, it was really disturbing."

This is what happens to trauma survivors who start to take on experiences and energy from the past; they become the damaged goods their abusive caregivers are projecting. Joe's mother's enmeshing abuse taught him to emotionally abandon himself to survive. He also learned that the result of relational connection, or being in relationship with a woman (such as his mother), is the loss of self, resulting in overwhelming feelings of entrapment and anger. The outgrowth becomes a perpetual cycle of living in destructive reaction, rather than engaging in corrective action toward the original trauma.

Post-traumatic Stress Disorder

To live in corrective action requires the reduction of the energy associated with traumatic wounding. The process of reducing the reaction or reactivity will begin, as with all recovery work, with awareness.

Mary sits across from me. She has contoured her body into a ball-like shape, her knees tucked under her like a camel resting in the shade. Her arms firmly embrace her torso, and her chin is seemingly glued to her neck. Tears stream down both cheeks.

As Mary begins to describe her emotional upset, she magically transforms into a childlike state. Her body goes limp, her eyes become distant and unfocused, and her breathing is shallow. It is as if she is literally reliving the brutal scene she begins to describe, experiencing all the terror her five-year-old body felt.

"What I remember is the sound," Mary says in a barely audible voice. "The sound of the strap hitting his raw skin—whap, whap, whap—then the low thud of my father's thick work boot kicking my eight-year-old brother's stomach, each kick pushing him across the floor," she says with a blank expression.

"I remember his eyes, too, the look of horror, like empty pools," she says as she tucks her head tighter to her chin. "And the blood. It splattered all over the wall when he kicked him in the nose." She is hiding behind her cupped hand, tears streaming down her face. The sadness that Mary has locked away for decades is released in retching waves of anguish.

Mary's father was a severe alcoholic; he had been an alcoholic for most of his life. Like many hearty Irish men, he preferred scotch as his demon of choice. Stopping at the neighborhood pub after his shift at the factory, he lived a cliché of Irish tradition.

"He was so wonderful when he didn't drink," Mary continues, her body relaxing ever so slightly. "He would take us with him on long drives, and I would feel like a princess." However, her fairy-tale world would end when he began to drink.

"What are you looking at, you little cunt?" her father would sneer. "You want a beating, too?"

"He looked possessed," Mary says. "My father became a monster." Tears continue to stream down her face.

"Where was your mom when this happened?" I ask.

"Cowering in the corner; what else could she do? We were all terrified."

When trauma templates are imprinted, the resulting response can develop into post-traumatic stress disorder (PTSD). This disorder is defined by a stressful occurrence "that is outside the range of usual human experience, and would be markedly distressful to almost anyone" (*Diagnosis Statistics Manual*). According to The Sidran Institute, PTSD has affected approximately 8 percent of all adults during their lives; that is one out of thirteen people in this country. It is often difficult to identify this disorder because our behaviors and reactions begin early in life, and this results in the normalization of one's reaction to the outside world.

How we react can take many forms, including:

- Hypervigilance
- Dissociation
- Intrusive thoughts, memories, flashbacks, or dreams
- Exaggerated startle response
- Constriction of body or breath
- Mood swings
- Poor affect regulation
- Disturbances in sleeping or eating patterns
- Amnesia or forgetfulness
- Compromised immune system

When clients seem to overreact to a seemingly benign experience, I point out their exaggerated response. I then coach them, helping them to create awareness of their own reactivity to specific events, people, places, and things. I also want them to be aware of any themes or clusters that might trigger their responses.

An effective gauge to monitor reactions is to evaluate them on a scale from one to ten, one being the mildest and ten the most severe response. I ask clients to rate how disturbing an occurrence feels; anything rated over three is usually linked to past trauma. The timing, intrusiveness, and repetition of the trauma determines the degree of the response.

The dramatic and profound effects of PTSD were documented by the Grant Study, conducted with 200 individuals who served in World War II. Each participant was re-interviewed forty-five years after he first described his experience. Individuals who did not experience PTSD had changed or altered their stories since the initial interviews; details had become less clear for them, and the emotional disturbances had less impact. The individuals who had PTSD did not alter their stories in the least. All of the details and descriptions were vividly recalled.

This is the norm for trauma survivors. The events can become imprinted or etched in the memory; when recall occurs, it is like rerunning a movie.

Mary sits in her bedroom, cowering as she hears the screen door slam and her father's footsteps come down the hall. Mary concentrates on the beam of afternoon light that filters in through her windows. She sees the dust particles dancing in the rays, suspended and weightless. In the distance, she hears her father clearing his throat and the familiar sound of the toilet seat lid being raised. The angle of the afternoon light indicates that he has come home early.

Her mother has gone to the store, her brother is out with friends, and Mary is alone with her father. Mary sits and stares, floating, suspended, becoming one with the particles. Running her finger through the rays, she watches them swirl, transporting herself into their world. Floating and swirling, she falls into a trancelike reverie.

No longer aware of her father, she is startled as the door to her bedroom abruptly opens. His pants still unhooked, her father slurs, "Oh, there you are, baby..." His gait is wobbly, his eyes are glassy, and his smell is revolting.

"I was looking for you, baby."

Mary's body tightens. "Hey, Daddy," she says, attempting to sound calm.

"What ya doing?" he purrs, petting her head with long strokes. "Come on over here," he says, moving his hands down her back.

The wretched smell of stale liquor is overwhelming as he pulls her closer. Mary knows that his hand will travel downward into her most private parts. She will feel the coarse skin of his fingers as he penetrates and probes. She will feel his arousal and his heavy breathing, and she will look at the rays of light, at the particles dancing and swirling, swirling and dancing.

How does a child like Mary survive her horrific destiny? How does a child emerge from such traumatic experiences and function as a healthy sexual being? Inherent in the human condition is the will to survive. The art of survival develops through a matrix of unconscious adaptations or coping mechanisms that are logistically layered intellectually, somatically, and emotionally.

Chapter 4

COPING WITH TRAUMA

Those who suffer from trauma must adapt or develop coping strategies in order to survive. These coping mechanisms can be broken down into eight categories: alarm reaction, somatic recall, intensity, numbing/satiation, shame binds, dissociation, deprivation, and destructive relationships.

Alarm Reaction

"I hate it when my boss comes back from lunch," Mary says, crinkling her nose and shaking her head. "He reeks of alcohol," she adds, sticking out her tongue as if she wants to vomit. "I feel nauseated; it makes me sick."

"It sounds like a strong reaction."

"Yeah, I hate alcohol on anybody's breath, but particularly his."

"Why do you think that is?"

"I don't know," she says defensively.

"Well, take a moment and think. Is there anything in your past that might be triggering your reaction?"

"Don't tell me," she looks up sheepishly. "You think it's because of my father."

"Who does your boss look like?"

Pausing in thought, she responds with a wry smile. "My dad."

"Does your reaction make sense?"

"*Yes*," she says.

What might be a normal, nonreactive experience for Mary's coworkers is a highly reactive situation for Mary because she is experiencing an alarm reaction. A severe and sudden post-traumatic stress reaction, an alarm reaction recalls the emotions associated with a traumatizing event of the past. One way in which an alarm reaction might manifest itself is in intrusive flashbacks. Often the person doesn't feel that he is living in the present; rather, he feels that he is constantly returning to the original trauma experience.

"I had a hard time seeing it," Mary continues, "but that makes sense. The smell makes me gag, and then I get a headache and it's hard to concentrate."

"Do you have this reaction when your boss doesn't smell of alcohol?"

"No. Otherwise, I like him; he's a really great boss."

"That is interesting because that is how you felt about your father."

"Oh, yeah," Mary says, making the connection.

Alarm reactions are often experienced as a total lack of control, as if the person is being robotically dominated by the emotion that has sprung from a traumatic past. When he is under the control of this emotion, the person lives in extremes. One extreme could be binging or acting out. The other extreme could be purging or restriction of behavior.

When the binging is over, the purge restores the sense of normality—without guaranteeing that another binge is on the horizon. The person is frightened and ashamed. Then a sense of hypervigilance takes over in order to provide the control necessary to avoid being hurled over the emotional cliff again.

Sitting in her bedroom, Mary looks at her reflection in the mirror. "I hate myself," she thinks. Mascara is smeared down her cheeks, her top is ripped to reveal her left shoulder, and her hair is in a massive, jumbled, matted mess. "I really hate myself," she repeats to herself.

That was not the case last night. Last night Mary was high. She was prepping for a binge. Mary knows the routine, a highly meticulous and ritualized process: Put on loud music; smoke cigarettes; shave legs; mousse hair; paint nails; apply lipstick; dab perfume; dress in a black miniskirt, stiletto heels, and low-cut top; and, of course, buy condoms.

"I just wanted to screw my brains out," Mary says. "I was on a rampage, a regular screw fest," she continues with more intensity in her voice.

"What triggered this binge?" I ask.

"I have no idea," she says, shrugging her shoulders.

"Well, it's important that we figure that out."

"Well, you tell me then," she says.

Mary came into therapy seeking treatment for her addiction to sex; she acted out with men, often in unsafe places with unknown parties. When the risk and danger were her high, it was an addiction she believed would ultimately kill her. The binges she began many years ago had progressed into more and more dangerous situations. Her binges could last several days, and they always ended in feelings of degradation and shame.

"Had something happened that you allowed yourself to be triggered?" I ask again.

"Yes," she says in a defeated tone. "That afternoon, my boss came up to explain the next phase of this project we were working on. I was standing over the renderings when he came up from behind, reeking of alcohol. He put his hand on my shoulder and slowly let his hand slide down my back. And then, inadvertently," she says, gesturing quotations with her fingers, "he brushes my ass. I was so shocked, I even second-guessed myself, like, 'Did that just happen?'—when I knew full well it did."

"This happened the same afternoon you acted out."

"Yes, I know. I had a bad reaction."

Mary's reaction is a typical adaptation aimed at alleviating the pain and horror of her past. Unfortunately, the reaction will unmercifully take Mary back into her shame core; it's the only way Mary has known how to cope.

Somatic Recall

Children who suffer from traumatic abuse before they are five years old do not have any powers of language or abstraction to place between themselves and the abuse. They cannot even say, "I was a bad boy" or "Mommy was in a bad mood." They have no words or theories to help them understand why they feel pain, fear, or shame. The only place for the sensation of abuse to land is on their bodies, and their bodies record the abuse as "somatic trauma." Like all trauma, it is stored and will be released when a later event triggers an analogy to the original abuse.

Even if the abused child has become an adult, the triggering of somatic trauma returns him to the young ego-state of his first infliction. The pain, fear, or shame is not felt as an idea or as something that can be talked about, but as a bodily sensation—what we call a "body memory." Helpless children have no cognitive control, and adults feel body memories as a child would: one-down, bewildered, disorganized, helpless. These early imprints are the most severe kinds of trauma, and the most difficult to treat, because they originate in preverbal wounding for which the therapist's language is incomprehensible.

When, in later life, persons with early wounding begin to work on their trauma issues, body memories may cause bewilderment, fear, and shame. These feelings can be so out of control that the adults experiencing them can believe they are going crazy.

I have watched people in group therapy react to other members of the group. When listening to another person's story, they become what we call "triggered." There are pockets of energy stored in our bodies. When something we sense—see, hear, smell, feel, or taste—"triggers" or opens up these pockets of memory, we get somatic recall. These body memories sometimes make people spontaneously start to cry. Sometimes their entire expressions and physical presentations change. They literally start to take on a frightened young child's appearance. Their shoulders slump, their faces become drawn and colorless, and they might even shake and begin to breathe shallowly. In this state, they are not able to articulate what they are experiencing. During this somatic (bodily) recall, energy that has been locked in the body is triggered and released.

I had not seen Mary for several weeks and, as I greet her, I notice that her usual vibrant, extroverted personality is withdrawn and tired. Barely able to make eye contact, she shuffles from the waiting room to my office as if weights are tied to her ankles. She collapses on the couch, grabbing a small pillow and clutching it to her abdomen as if it were a lifeline. Mary's head collapses as she lets out a loud sigh.

"I had a bad dream," Mary begins without even waiting for me to take my chair. "It was about my brother."

"Tell me what happened in the dream."

"He's been beaten so badly his guts and brains are spilling out. He is making a mess on the carpet. I am in a panic because I know my mother will be home and will be really angry if she sees the mess, but he keeps bleeding and I can't clean it up. Then I wake up in a cold sweat."

"When did you have this dream?" I ask.

"Two nights ago."

"You sound troubled by it still."

"I am. It has been a bad two days. I have had this severe nausea and headache, and I am afraid to fall asleep because I might have the dream again."

Mary was experiencing a somatic memory. The energy she had locked away and stored when she watched her brother being beaten was released when she had her dream. Mary's body had tensed up and become so tight that she virtually felt the pain in the same places the blows had struck her brother. It was as if she were carrying his pain.

This triggering of painful energy from the past is very typical in trauma survivors. The spontaneity of the emotions attached to these scenes can be disorienting. People like Mary don't know what is happening to them or why. As I said, people have told me that they believe they are going crazy.

Jenny, a tall and willowy woman in her late twenties, has been in treatment with me for several years. She is a trauma survivor who wears her scars well. Her sparkling blue eyes, dazzling smile, and sunny disposition mask her darkest childhood wounds. We have been working on her trauma for a year, but she seems discouraged today as she begins her session.

"I am so pissed off," Jenny says.

"Why is that?"

"Because I had another trip to the dentist."

"How did it go?"

"It was awful. I had to have him give me anesthesia to keep me calm, and that stuff always makes me feel sick."

"Is that what made you mad, your reaction to the anesthesia?"

"No, it's the fact that I had to have it," Jenny says in an exasperated voice.

Jenny's father was a sex offender. He had anally and orally penetrated her and ejaculated.

"Going to the dentist is always a painful experience," Jenny continues. "It always triggers painful body memories for me. It is almost unbearable for me to have my mouth forced open. It reminds me of my father forcing me to hold my mouth open to take in his penis. Sometimes I feel faint and dizzy. I see stars in front of my eyes. I have a gag reflex. Just having my teeth cleaned can be a traumatic and overwhelming feeling," she explains with a crunched-up face, dramatizing her disgust.

Jenny's discomfort is not limited to the dentist chair. Certain foods and textures have a similar triggering effect.

"It is impossible for me to eat tomato seeds because it reminds me of a similar texture in my father's ejaculate. It makes me gag. Also, I have a hard time eating peaches, and I refuse to put mangos and avocados in my mouth because I can't stand the textures."

But by far the most difficult somatic response for Jenny is a spontaneous body memory that she has been wrestling with for many years.

"Because I was anally penetrated, my bad dreams can trigger me to experience excruciating pain in my rectum. It feels as if someone is inserting a sharp poker. I break out into a cold sweat. One time I even fainted when I was trying to relieve myself to get rid of the pain. I did not know how I had gotten on the floor of the bathroom," she says, trailing off as if the memory is too painful to bear.

"It was very scary until I understood what was happening. I didn't know when some event, person, or place would trigger my body to respond like this. It would just hit me. It was like when I did not have control when my father would orally or anally rape me."

Jenny is not alone in her somatic responses. Like many sexual abuse survivors, she experiences body triggers. I like to explain the healing process to clients by noting that trauma is frozen in a person's body. The manner in which the body received the violations is imitated when the response is triggered. Jenny's gagging on tomato seeds or a dentist's drill recalls her gagging when she was orally raped. The traumatized body does not distinguish between her father's penis, the tomato seeds, and the dentist's instruments. Jenny's body knows only that something foreign is being forced into it, and its survival response is to gag it out. It is as if that part of her body "thawed" for a while and, once it was released, it froze back up, preserving the energy for another potential attack.

I explain to Mary and Jenny that the goal of treatment is to expel and dissipate the energy so it can no longer "thaw" under the instigation of a body memory and spread its traumatic poison. Through our work, we want to figuratively "melt" away the frozen body memory.

Intensity

The trauma-intensity pathway is formed when children are traumatized into associating intensity with pleasure. As adults, they can experience pleasure only when it is fused with intensity. People with hyperaroused intensity neuropathways probably grew up in extremely intense family environments. Perhaps the mother went into violent rages, or the father was a violent drunk.

The sexual acting-out behaviors associated with this kind of trauma usually carry high risk. They can include sadomasochism, exhibitionism, and prostitution. These behaviors trigger levels of chemical release that replicate the emotional ego-state of the trauma's original occurrence. This is part of the "rush." Often danger-intensity addicts are unable to orgasm except when danger and intensity are present. This trauma adaptation can affect other aspects of their lives; behaviors can range from not paying bills on time to jumping out of airplanes to having prostitutes in the house twenty minutes before the spouse returns home.

Twelve-year-old Ben sits on the rickety steps of the back porch. The back door opens, and he hears the familiar click of high heels descending the stairs. The smell of stale perfume wafts in his nostrils, a vivid reminder of the dead-end life his road-worn mother has chosen. Lighting up a cigarette, Ben looks out over the horizon, a barren, God-forsaken place he and his mother call home.

Ben's mother Lillie, once the belle of the county, now looks as tired and worn as the planks on which Ben rests. She joins Ben on the back porch, and he offers her his cigarette as if acting on a silent cue, a rehearsal they have practiced many times before. His mother's red, swollen lips take a long, slow drag, and she passes it back.

Lillie married young to a violent alcoholic who left her and her infant son less than a year into their marriage. Working two jobs, Lillie put herself through nursing school and, upon graduation, secured a position at the local hospital.

Despite Lillie's advanced academic studies, she had yet to graduate to a successful relationship. A series of alcoholic, drug-addicted men who beat her and left her yielded a cynical, jaded woman who used narcotics as the prescription to ease her broken heart. After getting hooked on and ultimately caught stealing her patients' drugs, Lillie became unemployed, with a suspended nursing license.

Desperate to survive, Lillie became a prostitute, her place of work a seedy, dilapidated building housing a dozen or so women with a steady stream of male patrons. Ben, only six at the time, became a familiar visitor, because he preferred the company of the doting women to the empty, one-room apartment his mother rented down the street.

When Ben visited his mother, he was met by women in cheap polyester robes that outlined the shapes of their sagging bosoms and exposed the secrets between their aging thighs. Ben was initiated into the sordid sexual hell to which his mother had been condemned.

At the age of thirteen, Ben found his mother dead in their apartment, lying in a pool of her own blood. She had been shot by her drug-crazed boyfriend. Ben quickly left the back roads of Idaho, hitching rides to Los Angeles. Ben, well-trained in the power of sexual favors, did whatever he needed to get whatever he wanted.

Now a man of thirty-five, Ben is a cop in the most dangerous neighborhoods of downtown L.A.

"I crave the action of the street," Ben says. "I feel safer there than any other place. It's what I know. It's where I feel most comfortable." His calls take him into familiar situations that reinforce the history he has endured.

"I don't feel alive unless I am around danger."

"Is that true sexually?" I ask.

"Absolutely," he says. "I can't even get turned on unless there is some kind of risk," he explains.

Ben had become familiar with an environment in which life and death always hung in the balance. His brain's release of chemicals, such as adrenaline, dopamine, and serotonin, make him feel alive.

For Ben, a moderate lifestyle is not only intolerable, but also unimaginable. His body craves a much higher level of intensity. So Ben works in the most dangerous part of his city, where each situation could mean life or death. Ben describes himself as a "pit bull," and he has won respect among his peers because of the high level of intensity he can tolerate. He is like a drinker with a high tolerance for alcohol.

Ben enters these dangerous situations feeling calm and at ease. "I always felt cocksure," Ben says. "It's what I knew, and I loved it."

To relieve the stress from the chemicals he infuses into his body, Ben engages in a form of numbing or satiation that allows him to "come down" off the high.

Numbing/Satiation

Intensity addicts commonly wind up with satiation as the counterreaction to their chemical high. Addicts live an "all or nothing" kind of life. This is certainly true for

Ben, who does not know how to moderate himself. Ben knows only two ways to live: either full-out pedal-to-the-metal or completely numb.

In order to block the pain of early trauma, people like Ben stuff themselves with various substances and/or engage in activities to the point of numbness. They are trying to obliterate shameful, painful emotions over which they have no other control. Some of these compulsively excessive behaviors are overeating, sleeping, television, reading, electronic game playing, Internet use (sometimes sexual, but not always), and using depressive drugs such as alcohol.

When Ben comes home from work, he lifts weights and runs like a demon. He lifts for at least an hour and runs for at least an hour every day. He also practices the martial arts. It takes his mind off all the intensity he experiences on his shift. But his demon workouts also maintain a sustenance level of adrenaline, endorphins, and serotonin, which sustain his high. This excessive workout routine makes him feel strong enough to protect himself in the intense and dangerous environment he has created, in which he feels safe and calm. But after he works out, he uses numbing as a depressant drug.

Ben is basically creating a chemical cocktail in his brain so that he can sleep and "relax." But, because of the high emotional and neurological levels that he has created for himself, he isn't able to come down without the aid of some kind of satiating drug. Ben's drug is pot. He smokes a joint or two every night. Even though he is a health nut, he justifies smoking dope by saying he is not "out of control" and it helps to relax him. So Ben is alternately living in two extremes: fear/danger/intensity or satiety/numbness.

Shame

When pain and pleasure become fused in the furnace of profound shame, they often yield the sexual perversion of sadomasochism, which is an acting-out behavior that has at its core the shame-existence bind.

Richard von Krafft-Ebing coined the term *masochism* after it had become a prevalent literary motif in early nineteenth-century literature. The era was marked by a family system in which the father was often the punishing lord and master, the grandiose and severe inflicter of painful discipline. The literary work in which nineteenth-century masochism was most notoriously dramatized was von Sacher-Masoch's novel *Venus in Furs* (1870). Krafft-Ebing defines masochism as:

. . . a peculiar perversion of the psychical sexual life in which the individual affected, in sexual feelings and thought, is controlled by the idea of being completely and unconditionally subject to the will of a person of the opposite sex: of being treated by this person as by a master, humiliated and abused. This idea is colored by lustful feelings; the masochist lives in fantasies, in which he creates situations of this kind and often attempts to realize them.

Here the individual's destructive attitude turns inward on himself instead of outward on his original abuser, often the father against whom he could not retaliate when he was a child. He is involved in a perverse and self-destructive attempt to gain the power and control he lacked as an abused child. By investing pain with erotic pleasure, he mocks the threat that his original painful discipline was intended to achieve, thus "undoing the abuse." The masochist, by accepting self-punishment, secretly repudiates his parental abuser, because the beating is subliminally directed at him.[1]

These shame-based people are challenging to treat because just talking about and stirring the embers of memory is often too painful to bear. They immediately experience a sense of self-loathing so intolerable that they crawl behind a wall in order to survive the unbearable feelings. Often the shame is so deep they experience what Pia Mellody calls the "shame-existence bind," wherein the person doesn't think that he is worthy even to take up space on this planet. He does not think that he is worthy of the act of healing.

People whose shame-existence bind leads them to self-destructive, sexual acting-out behaviors are dramatic examples of how sexual deviancy seeks to "undo" the original abuse by taking power and control. There is no better example of the operation of the furnace of "carried shame" than that exemplified in masochism. The shame the child carried for the abusive parent has fused so completely with his own identity that he takes revenge on himself in order to take revenge on his shamer.

[1] Kaja Siverman, *Male Subjectivity at the Margins* (New York: Routledge, 1992), p. 185.

Peter had a mother who shamed him verbally, not only one on one, but in front of his peers at school and at family gatherings. She told him that he was stupid and that he didn't know what he was doing. She said he was ugly and that she wished she had given birth to a daughter rather than a son.

At family gatherings, Peter's aunt, who was only five years older, would suggest that they play in the back shed. In the shed, Peter's aunt would tie him up and perform oral sex on him. When he became an adult, Peter believed that women would degrade him and put him down. With this template embedded in his brain, he habitually visited prostitutes, requesting S and M (sadomasochistic) behaviors. Dominatrices would tie him up, abuse him verbally, and hit him. He would request oral sex. These needs were evidence of the shame, intensity, and fear of the wounds inflicted by his mother and his aunt.

These sadomasochistic scenes grew more and more intense and dangerous, driven by Peter's need to reinforce the shaming messages he received as a child.

Dissociation

One way the immaturely parented child can adapt to abuse is to fly off into fantasy so that he doesn't have to look reality in the eye. He dissociates himself from painful information because he has come to believe the falsehood his caregivers have taught him: that he is worthless. From the one-down position, he chooses to live in the shut-down world of his adaptation rather than face the reality that he does not deserve his place on the planet. He creates fantasies in which he has power and control. Trapped within the dysfunction of this kind of trauma, he chooses isolation, so that he is free to create his own world rather than risk contact with reality.

Even worse off than the love addict who turns a *real-life* lover into "a knight in shining armor," the individual suffering from trauma dissociation eschews real people and substitutes a dream world of his own making. In the world of sexual deviation, this is the realm of romance novel addicts and the fictitious re-creation of self in Internet chat rooms.

Trauma dissociation protects the traumatized individual from learning information that is too shameful for him to accept. It is a challenge to treat this particular kind of trauma because trauma dissociation is so effective. The individual creates almost impregnable compartments in which he locks away his "bad news" so that it cannot escape and damage his self-esteem. The degradation is kept separate from all other information in his life.

❖ ❖ ❖ ❖

When Sally made her first appointment for therapy, she emphatically explained that she was in relationship crisis and needed help. A woman in her early thirties, Sally seemed confident, articulate, and eager to get to work.

"I fell in love with my dance instructor," Sally begins. "He is an unbelievable dancer," she continues.

"You said there are problems in the relationship."

"Well, sort of."

"Tell me what is going on."

"Well, the problem is he doesn't know I love him."

"Have you told him?" I ask.

"Oh, no! NO, NO, NO!"

"What's the resistance?"

"Well, he doesn't even know I like him. I mean, we are friendly, but we only do things in groups."

"You're dating?" I ask, perplexed.

"No," she says, pausing. "Not yet."

Sally's "relationship" took place in her head. A fantasy became a 24/7 IV drip. As I explore the nature of Sally's fantasy, I discover it is a highly developed one.

"I have photos of him on the walls in my bedroom," Sally explains. "I even had him sign them."

For the last year, Sally had been fanning the flames of her addiction into a heated and painful obsession. The fantasy had grown in power to the point at which she started following him. She would drive by his house in order to spy on him. She told me that this escape she was creating in her mind felt as if she were taking a shot of heroin. There was immense pleasure and excitement. There was relief from pain and discomfort.

Despite all this, Sally is not interested in pursuing any real relationship. Her emotional satisfaction takes place in this world of fantasy. By keeping her feelings secret, she can maintain her fantasy for herself. That way, she believes that she has power and control. She can have a secret world that operates just as she wants it to.

The roots of Sally's problem lie in how isolated she had been as a child. She spent almost all of her time alone, until fantasy became her only friend. Fantasy replaced the real world. She crawled into these cocoonlike compartments that reduced her distress. Fantasy became her drug of choice.

Individuals who suffer from multiple addictions often find that these addictions interchange or replace one another. The clients deposit their shame into separate addictive compartments, each driven by a different addictive remedy (drugs, alcohol, sex, gambling). The dysfunctional purpose of dissociation is to allow the traumatized individual to continue indulging his addiction in one place, while banking the self-esteem of having stopped it in another.

An example of this is the alcoholic who becomes sober. Once he is in recovery from alcohol abuse, he starts acting out sexually. He holds sobriety for alcohol and sexual acting-out in two separate compartments and may not talk about the still-active addiction for years. When I treat a person who has revealed multiple active addictions, such as sex, eating, and gambling, I treat one at a time, giving priority to the addiction most likely to destroy him.

Deprivation

Trauma deprivation is rooted in profound shame, and the deprivation the person imposes on himself is punishment for being unworthy. The deprivation can be imposed on any part of a person's life, such as money, sex, food, work, or social relations. Such a person seeks to gain power and control by taking no risks that would result in exposure of his addiction. This individual is not only afraid, but horrified at the thought of being sexual.

✧ ✧ ✧ ✧

Lisa, a woman in her mid-fifties, has been working with me for almost a year. She has been in several relationships but reports that being sexual is "difficult."

"What do you mean by difficult?" I ask.

"I dread being sexual," she answers. "I find it almost intolerable."

Lisa's reaction is a typical response for a person with sexual aversion. The idea of being sexual can cause marked distress, including headaches, dissociation, nausea, anxiety or panic attacks, flashbacks, intrusive thoughts, and body memories.

Like many people who suffer from sexual aversion, Lisa is an expert in avoiding an act she has come to dread. She is an attractive woman; however, she wears baggy clothing that successfully hides her body. She cannot afford to call attention to her figure or have anyone find her attractive.

When Lisa does enter a relationship, she maintains an arsenal of strategies that allow her to avoid being sexual: she has a headache, she doesn't feel well, it's that time of the month, she's too busy, she starts an argument, she goes to bed early, she goes to bed late, or she initiates physical contact at inappropriate moments, such as before company arrives or before she has to leave for work. The planning and execution of the avoidance are just as powerful and consuming as the acting-out behavior, but the goals are opposite.

Like the acting-out side of the cycle, aversion is usually based in traumatic wounding. This is true for Lisa.

Lisa lies in the vacant king-sized bed while her dad

readies himself for sleep. It is Lisa's job to "warm it up" and then "snuggle" with her dad before she scurries off to her own room for the night. Lisa's mother, a nurse who works the late shift, won't be home for at least a few hours. Lisa lies in bed, tightly tucked under the covers. The lights out in the bedroom, Lisa watches the adjoining bathroom as her dad passes by the door, getting ready. As her dad is clad in boxer shorts made of thin cotton fabric, Lisa can see, by the backlight, a view of her father's genitals. Seeing her father this way has become normal for Lisa.

"You know, I never thought of that as being bad or inappropriate," Lisa says.

"Do you think it affected you?"

"I never did until I realized that seeing your father mostly naked is shocking for a kid. I don't think he did it on purpose, but it surely imprinted my sexual development and affected my discomfort with my own body."

Lisa's father's lack of boundaries became even more intrusive once he pulled back the covers and joined Lisa in the bed.

"I remember him wrapping his arms around me to start, and then his hands would begin to wander. He would rub my back, then slip his hands under my pajamas, rubbing my butt, and then he would make his way to my genitals."

"What was that like for you, when something that was supposed to be nurturing turned into sexual trauma?"

"It was confusing. I loved my dad, and I wanted to be close to him and make him happy. But something inside of me knew it was wrong, but, at the same time, it felt good. I think the hardest part was feeling frozen, like I had no control."

Lisa's imprinting of sexual abuse has kept her from having healthy sexual relationships. Even the thought of being touched can set off an intense emotional reaction.

"I only like to be touched if I feel in control," Lisa explains. "I don't even like to be around people who are being affectionate."

"Why is that?" I ask.

"Because I feel uncomfortable. I see them as being weak, unable to control themselves."

"So when you are in a relationship, there is no show of public affection?"

"We'll hold hands, but that's about it," she says, shrugging her shoulders.

"What about in private?"

"It's easier in private, as long as I feel I am in control."

"What does that look like, being in control?"

"I have to have my eyes open, lights on, facing the person."

"Are you able to experience pleasure?"

"Sometimes."

"Are you able to orgasm?"

"Never," Lisa says with defiance.

Lisa's level of sexual aversion is extreme. It is a terror traumatically imprinted in her core. When this fear is triggered, it takes her back to the scared, helpless little girl lying frozen in her father's bed.

Destructive Relationships

The emotional bonds we make under the provocation of traumatic wounds are always dysfunctional, often involving us with people who are dangerous, shaming, or exploitative. A person believes she is in a relationship for something like love or companionship. In truth, her inappropriate, abusive partner reminds her of her familiar basis in shame. She stays in dangerous, destructive situations because she subliminally finds that the abuse makes her feel right at home. It was dangerous growing up and acting like a wounded child trying to get loved. It will remain dangerous being an adult wounded child trying to get love. The results will be the same. Addicts will get what they still crave from their original abusers: shame from "adult" relationships.

Beth is thirty-five and very thin, weighing only about 100 pounds; her face is hollow and pale. Her legs are drawn tightly against her chest in a fetal position. She is unwilling to make eye contact with me as she tells me her story.

She was sexually abused by her father and raped several times in her adult life. She was married and had a daughter, whom her husband abused sexually. He admitted this abuse to the authorities. Beth and her husband were separated and, yet, after a while, she let him back in the house. He told her that the problem was hers and that, if she weren't so depressed, things would work out. Beth eventually entered treatment, but she was so rooted in her denial about her husband's behavior that she left her child alone with him in the house.

As she sits across from me in the fetal position, she finally makes eye contact. She has piercing eyes. She says, "What I need to know, Maureen, is can I trust him?"

I look at her, cup my hands around my mouth, and say as loudly as I can, "No!" And then I say loudly, spacing out each word with staccato emphasis: "He is a perpetrator!" I am trying to shock her back into reality, to break through her denial. If Beth is unable to break through, she will be unable to heal.

Trauma is a profound experience that affects all aspects of our lives. In his book *Waking the Tiger*, Peter Levine describes trauma's impact and the possibilities it solicits:

Trauma is a fact of life. It does not, however, have to be a life sentence. Not only can trauma be healed but also, with appropriate guidance and support, it can be transformative. "Trauma has the potential to be one of the most significant forces for psychological, social, and spiritual awakening and evolution. How we handle trauma (as individuals, communities, and societies) greatly influences the quality of our lives. It ultimately affects how or even whether we will survive as a species."

Chapter 5

SEXUALIZED ANGER

Healthy sexual desire is nourished by love, connectivity, and intimacy. However, when we have been traumatized into compulsive sexuality, love, connectivity, and intimacy are replaced by shame. As we have already discussed, sexualized anger is the reaction to the shame that trauma fosters. Let's consider the model below.

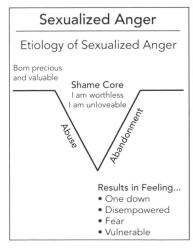

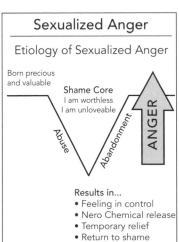

We are all born with inherent worth and value. But when we grow up in abusive and abandoning environments; are told we are worthless; and are physically, sexually, verbally, emotionally, and intellectually abused by our caregivers, we are compelled to believe that we are worthless and not deserving. In order to survive these painful beliefs and feelings, we mask them with anger. Anger masks our shame so that we do not have to recognize the ego-annihilating pain that lies behind it. When new clients come into my office and share their histories, I listen first for the shame and, second, for their reaction to the shame, the mask of anger.[2]

Three-year-old Ben stands at the gate and cries. Barely able to see over the top of the wooden child gate locked in place, he can see his mother working in the backyard. His anxious cries become louder as he shakes and pulls on the gate. Ben's mother ignores him. He throws his body down on the wooden floor. Ben kicks at the gate and cries, gasping for air. His mother throws down the trowel she has been using to tend to her flower beds and sighs. By the time she reaches the doorway and is

---

[2]Not all anger is dysfunctional. Healthy anger gives us the strength to protect ourselves from physical and emotional harm. Anger becomes dysfunctional when we mistake the harm we are doing to ourselves, or when another's behavior triggers our own sense of worthlessness, making us vulnerable to an attack from outside. The anger we feel toward that outside person is the projection of the shame we feel at our own worthlessness. Because it feels empowering to be angry and disempowering to be shamed, we choose

towering over him, Ben has stopped crying. Her stare is stern as she narrows her eyes and purses her lips. "You are a selfish, selfish boy," she says. The words pierce Ben's heart like arrows. "A selfish boy," she repeats. Ben lies on the floor, looking up at his mother. He sees the displeasure in her eyes as she leaves him behind.

His cries turn to whimpers. Defeated, he makes his way over to the couch, lying face down. Unable to articulate his pain, he deliberately drools on the expensive fabric.

"If I can't have her, I will destroy her couch," he thinks. Ben cannot put his revenge into so many words, but his actions speak for his three-year-old feelings.

Of all the instinctual drives of childhood, I believe the one most often left unidentified (perhaps because it is so obvious) is the obsession for the familiar. Children have an instinctual need to belong to a life-sustaining family system, but this survival trait has a design flaw. Children continue to obsess for the familiar, even when the familiar harms rather than nurtures. Even if parenting becomes abusive, children choose to fit and adjust rather than protest and risk ostracism. They are hardwired to believe that abandonment must be avoided, no matter the cost. Ben will passively and aggressively express his anger at his mother, disguising it enough so that she will not leave him totally unprotected.

Just before dawn Ben creeps downstairs, not daring to awaken anyone. The pads on the bottom of his Dr. Dentons grip the polished hardwood floors as he rounds the corner into the kitchen. Flipping on the light, he is temporarily blinded. The kitchen, like the rest of the house, is large and formal. The countertops and the imported Italian marble floors reflect the recessed ceiling lights.

The rumbles of Ben's stomach have driven him out of his warm bed. Knowing it is too early to wake anyone, Ben decides to make his first-ever breakfast for himself. Scooting the heavy wooden chair across the floor, Ben is careful not to make a sound. This is an arduous task because the chair weighs half as much as Ben does. But the pride Ben is feeling at his independence forestalls any misgivings.

Placing the chair under the cabinet, Ben carefully climbs up. He reaches for the familiar red-and-white box and his ceramic blue bowl. Gingerly he sets them down on the counter as he lowers himself onto the floor.

Pulling on the refrigerator door, he retrieves the milk and sets it on the counter next to the bowl. Ben climbs back up on the chair as he begins to tilt the cereal box ever so slightly. He then shakes the contents into his bowl. But, as he shakes a little harder, the contents gain momentum and spill out over the sides of his bowl, rolling over the counter and onto the floor. Deciding he can clean up later, Ben reaches for the milk. The weight and cumbersome shape of the gallon container make it impossible for Ben to maneuver. It slips out of his hands, bounces off the counter, makes a loud thud, splits open, and gushes all over the floor. Just as Ben is climbing down to attend to the mess, his mother rounds the corner.

"What are you doing?" she screeches. "Look at the mess you are making! It's five o'clock in the morning, and I'll never get back to sleep. All you can think of is yourself."

Ben's big blue eyes are fixed on his mother, who grabs the broom and begins hitting and shooing Ben out of the kitchen.

For Ben, an only child, his mother's reactions to his immature and youthful imperfections remain constant over the years—until he stops trying to please her.

It is an awful irony that the trauma we receive from being abused becomes the dysfunctional guarantee that, for the rest of our lives, we will be emotionally unable to leave the family that has abused us. Trauma, in the form of post-traumatic stress reaction, guarantees that we will always have our place at the psychic table where we were poisoned. Memories of the abusive family will shame us, and anger will be our defensive reaction.

Ben's mother, incapable of nurturing her child, leaves him feeling worthless, unwanted, and shamed. The painful message he receives from her is, "I don't want you. You are a burden. Leave me alone." A young child can't reason that rejection by his mother is due to her limited emotional resources. Instead, he internalizes the abandonment as being his fault; he believes, "There is something inherently wrong with *me.*" When the precious part of a person is no longer nurtured but is damaged through abuse and abandonment, this creates "the shame core." At the core of who we are, we believe we are worthless and irreparably flawed.

We are born precious and valuable, even though our humanity has its physical and emotional limitations. To accept this perfect imperfection is the essence of the healthy ego-state. Whatever imperfections we have, they are part of our humanity—facts not to be despised, feared, or railed against. Our imperfections remind us that we are not gods, that we are humans among other humans, each with his set of strengths and weaknesses. We have work to do if we are to maximize the good and minimize the bad. This self-affirming correction is a joy, considering that the payoff is healthy self-esteem and social comfort.

However, abuse and abandonment can erode our sense that we are precious and valuable. We begin to define ourselves by our flaws. Abuse can take many forms: physical, emotional, neglect, sexual, spiritual, and intellectual. When our caregivers do not teach us or support us in accepting our perfect imperfection, they have abandoned their primary responsibility to us. It is fair to call such parental failure "abandonment."

We can be abandoned in many ways. Abandonment can include a parent's leaving, illness, or death. It can result from overt abuse such as violence and demeaning verbal attacks.

"I'm going to get you," Ben hears his nanny say as she enters the room. Hiding under the floor-length tablecloth, Ben holds his breath and body still. "I'm going to find you," she says as she abruptly lifts the cloth, revealing the giggling little boy.

"I got you," she says, pulling him out and lifting him up, tickling his rounded tummy. Ben's eyes dance with joy as she continues tickling him, saying in a singsong cadence, "I got you."

Nanny is a large woman with an ample figure. She is a stark contrast to Ben's petite, slim, tailored mother. Nanny's low voice oozes out like warm syrup pouring over steamy hotcakes. Her laugh is hearty and deep, and her eyes are warm and inviting.

Nanny came to work for the family as soon as Ben was brought home from the hospital. Being close to Nanny always felt safe to Ben. With his mother, whose mood swings alternated between coldness and aggression, Ben learned to be warily anxious. But Ben loved to be held by Nanny. He felt cocooned in her large warm body, comforted as he rested his head on her soft breast, lulled by the rise and fall of her breathing and the tone of the songs she hummed.

Ben's only other confidante and companion was his dog, Freckles. Ben's family lived in upstate New York on fifteen acres of heavily wood hillsides, with a wide creek and pond. Beyond the front door, green trees and open fields became the canvas for Ben's imagination. Floating down the creek, he became Tom Sawyer or a pirate looking for hidden treasures. Freckles was on the lookout as they foraged through the woods, watchful for hostile Indians or robbers eager to steal their gold. When the day was through, Freckles curled up, head on Ben's legs, as they drifted into a sound sleep.

Freckles walked Ben to the school bus each morning and greeted him in the afternoon. Ben fed and groomed him, and, in return, Freckles was a faithful lifeline that eased Ben's cavernous pain. Like Ben, Freckles was a feisty spirit, always running and jumping, ready to play at any opportunity.

The long, sloping front yard was a place for games of fetch the Frisbee, sponge footballs, and sticks. Freckles chased them all until one fall afternoon when Ben threw a

high, long pass, which rolled down the hill and into the
street. Freckles was off at high speed, running over the crest
of the hill and down to the street. After hearing a screech
of tires, a low thud, and the slam of a car door, Ben knew
his faithful friend was gone.

Little comfort was offered by his parents. "He was a
dog, for Christ's sake," Ben's father bellowed. "This crying
and moping around the house has got to stop. You're
upsetting your mother." The only connection Ben had
had with warmth and nurturing was with Nanny, and he
had long outgrown her cuddles and hugs.

Several days later, Ben was no less distraught. Alone on
a rainy Sunday afternoon, Ben aimlessly rambled around
the empty house. He listened to the staccato sound of the
rain hitting the roof, and the gray light filtering in
through the windows only compounded his sadness.

Wandering into Nanny's quarters, he glanced at the
photos that adorned her dresser; he lay on her bed and
breathed in her smell. He wrapped himself in her
comforter, remembering her embrace. Ben relaxed for
the first time since the death of Freckles.

Drifting off into a light slumber, Ben was jolted by a
loud clap of thunder. Groggy, he sat up and noticed one of
Nanny's bras draped over a doorknob. Intrigued, Ben
unwrapped himself from the warmth of the comforter and
reached for the undergarment. He observed its functional
design, so different from any of the frilly, scantily designed
undergarments he had seen in the *Playboy* magazines his
Dad kept stashed in the basement. He caressed the bra
against his cheek; it felt soothing and comforting, but also

wrong. Being so close to something so intimate of Nanny's felt naughty, but it also felt titillating.

Despite Ben's recognition that he had violated Nanny's privacy, he was unable to stop. He knew it was wrong, but, even worse, he was enjoying it. An overwhelming urge overtook him and, in that moment, Ben made a decision that changed his life. He stole Nanny's bra. He violated his core values, but he could not help himself. The relief was too great.

Ben's ritual of stealing Nanny's bras and masturbating with them lasted for years. It was his first sexual "high."

Ben's compulsive behaviors fused shame and fear with sexual arousal. Ben's mother taught him that needing or wanting love and attention was "selfish." Ben learned that his emotional dependence on her led to shaming words, which cut him to his core. His nanny had provided for some of his emotional needs, but her succor came too late to overcome the traumatic damage caused by his mother. He had already learned his traumatic lesson: Do not trust anyone, especially women.

Ben's father also taught through example: Provide superficial comfort for your woman so that she will leave you alone, then retaliate by stealing away to your secret stash of *Playboy* magazines in the basement.

When Ben began to steal bras, he was acting out his anger: anger against what his mother was incapable of giving him, and the shame and pain of his traumatically induced worthlessness. Nanny, as his mother-substitute, received this deflected anger.

Sexualized anger can be passive-aggressive, as it was when Ben stole Nanny's bras and masturbated, or it can be fully aggressive and overt. All sexual acting-out, however, is motivated by feelings of shame and is manifested in acts and feelings of anger.

Ben married a woman who was very attentive to his needs and wants. She was expressive, emotional, and present to him emotionally. In the first few years of his marriage, Ben was happy. He and his wife enjoyed fulfilling, tender, and nurturing lovemaking. She listened to Ben's worries and problems, giving supportive and useful suggestions. In the mornings, they snuggled, and, in the evenings, they took long walks in the wooded hillsides. Both were eager to start a family and, when their firstborn turned out to be twins, they were thrilled. The two little girls had bright blue eyes and dimples that matched their father's.

Ben knew little about caring for newborns. In his family of origin, that lesson was never modeled. Middle-of-the-night feedings left his wife exhausted and emotionally detached. He watched his little girls receiving much of the attention once reserved for him. Secretly, Ben was jealous. Not being cared for aroused familiar feelings deep in his psyche. That is the way his mother had made him feel.

Ben began having anxiety attacks. It was difficult for him to sleep and eat, but mostly Ben felt angry. "What about me?" he thought, resenting the bond between mother and daughters. "What happened to my loving, adoring wife?"

Ben began to spend more time at the office. His anger continued to simmer until finally it exploded. "If she doesn't have time for me anymore, I'll find someone who does!" he thought. That afternoon, Ben went to his first massage parlor.

Walking into the seedy, dark foyer, Ben pushed down any feelings of fear or guilt. He was guided along the narrow hallway, his head buzzing, his breath shallow, his heart pounding. When Ben entered the small, dimly lit room, he was oblivious to the dank smell, the sleazy surroundings, and even the woman who stood in front of him. Ben was high.

Much to Ben's surprise, he wanted only one thing, and it wasn't sex. He wanted this stranger to hold him against her large, warm bosom and hum to him. When she did, Ben let out a long sigh and finally was able to relax.

Once again, Ben was in the emotional bosom of his childhood nanny. But along with the return to Nanny came the anger implicit in the association of sexual pleasure with the forbidden. And along with the forbidden came the shame of the transgression. Like an alcoholic who, after a period of sobriety, takes that next drink, the doors of addiction swung wide open for Ben. Pleasure and shame were his heady cocktail, and he would subconsciously pursue them both with greater and greater intensity.

Soon Ben's sexual acting out became more blatant and dangerous. He would have unprotected sex with strange women. He invited a trick back to his home and got rid of her just seconds before his wife walked in the door. He spent large sums on prostitutes, heedless that his spending would be easy to discover. Sexuality was now fused with danger, as if Ben were inviting disgrace for being the shameful, disgraced person he believed he was.

Ben had been in an alarm reaction since the birth of the twins, when he imagined that his wife's diversion of attention from him to the children was similar to his mother's abandonment of him. He had been jolted back in time to memories of his childhood. His wife was transformed into his mother, and the resentment, anger, and rage he had harbored for so many years erupted into a binge lasting several years.

It wasn't until Ben's wife investigated unusual charges on their monthly credit-card statement that Ben ended up in my office.

"Why do you go to prostitutes?" I ask.

"Because I can't get what I want from my wife," he says with a slight tone of indignation.

"What is it that you want?"

"A little attention would be nice," he says in a sarcastic tone.

"Have you asked for that?"

"What's the use? After our third child was born, I knew I could kiss it goodbye."

"Kiss what goodbye?"

"Any attention from her," he says, his body melting into a defeated ball.

"How old do you feel right now?" I ask.

"I don't know," he says in an agitated tone.

"Well, check in with yourself because your body and facial expression look very young."

Ben lets out a sigh of exasperation, as if this type of introspection is beneath him.

"I guess about three," he says, rolling his eyes.

"Three years old," I repeat.

"Um hmm."

"Well, that is a problem because I can't work with a three-year-old; I need to work with your adult."

Ben's forehead furrows, and he narrows his eyes as if to center me in the crosshairs of a rifle: "What in the *hell* are you talking about?"

"You look confused," I say.

"Yeah, just a little," he says, even more exasperated.

"Well, let me float my idea by you, and you see if it fits."

Ben says nothing but lets me continue.

"When your children were born, I believe you had a traumatic response that propelled you back to your original wounding, the abandonment by your mother. This triggered feelings of shame, which were intolerable, and so you moved to anger—sexual anger—to ease your pain, and you acted out."

"Makes sense," Ben says, barely nodding his head.

"If we overlay the original coping mechanism over your acting-out behaviors, they are exactly the same, right down to the remaking of Nanny—same body type, same behavior."

"Hmm . . . interesting," Ben says, making the connection. "So what do we do?" he asks with more hope in his voice.

"That's easy. First you get sober, and next we heal your shame core."

"Can we do that by the end of the week?" he says with a wry smile and chuckle.

"Sorry, but I think it might take a bit longer than that."

Healing core wounds is a process that requires diligent work and commitment. Often the process feels overwhelming, but the rewards are worth the struggle.

Ben was one of those clients willing to dig in and stay the course. Although his marriage ended in divorce, he found a sense of peace and connection with himself that he'd never dreamed possible. Ben was able to address his deep-seated anger and heal his shame in healthy ways (the specifics of which we will discuss in later chapters). Ben no longer needed to use his sexualized anger to cover his shame core.

Sexual addiction has primarily been seen as a male disorder; this is due to the cultural stereotype that sex addicts are, among other things, perverted, deviant, or oversexed men. Given this perception, identifying women as sex addicts is often perceived, both in personal and professional realms, as inapplicable.

Further complicating this diagnostic block is the fact that the mental health field does not officially recognize sexual addiction as a mental "disorder," meaning it is not listed in the *Diagnostic Statistical Manual of Mental Disorders-IV* (*DSM-IV*), the manual used to diagnose or evaluate individuals' behaviors.

Without a "legitimized" diagnosis for sexual addiction, some mental health practitioners question its validity. This situation leaves the possibility that those who are suffering will not be diagnosed or treated for their disease—a disease that can be fatal.

The diagnostic criteria most commonly used by those who treat sexual addiction are similar to those applied to chemical dependence. They include:

- **Loss of Control.** Clear behaviors that go further than intended, such as having unprotected sex, meeting someone as opposed to just talking to them online, and having sex in dangerous conditions, such as with a coworker in the office storage area during business hours.
- **Compulsive Behaviors.** A pattern of out-of-control behaviors over time, such as masturbating to the point of injury.
- **Efforts to Stop.** Failed attempts to stop the behaviors, such as broken promises to self or others, or bargaining with oneself (e.g., "I will only *flirt* with someone at the bar instead of having sex").
- **Losses.** Significant losses due to engaging in behaviors related to acting out sexually (e.g., sacrificing hobbies, commitments, and financial, career, and family obligations; not meeting deadlines; or forgetting special occasions).
- **Preoccupation.** Obsessing about behaviors, leaving the addict disengaged or disconnected from the present moment. This allows for emotional numbing but will never provide or promote personal intimacy or connection with others.
- **Progression.** The need to make the behavior more intense, frequent, or risky. Like an alcoholic, the sex addict will reach a threshold or plateau that needs to be amplified in order to maintain the desired high.

- **Continued Behavior despite Negative Consequences.** The inability to stop a behavior that creates problems, including legal, physical, financial, or relational problems. The addict is usually in a great deal of denial as to the extent to which his addiction has permeated his life.
- **Withdrawal.** Stopping behavior causes physical and/or emotional discomfort or distress, including mood swings, depression, irritability, headaches, nausea, dissociation, interrupted sleep patterns, anxiety, or intrusive thoughts.

It is hoped and anticipated that the subsequent edition of the *DSM* will include sexual addiction as an official disorder. This will enable those working in the healing profession to first identify and then facilitate treatment.

Another limitation is the paucity of research in the field of sexual addiction. Research has been primarily conducted with males and limited to those in treatment facilities. Although this information has been vitally important, the limited population leaves questions as to how many populations are being unidentified or misidentified.

Dr. Patrick Carnes, a pioneer in the field of sexual addiction, discovered that, after a ten-year study, an estimated 6 to 8 percent of males and 3 percent of females are sexually addicted. I believe the actual numbers, especially for the female population, to be much higher. This is not to discount the work of those who have provided vital statistical information, but rather to question

and challenge their conclusions so that further
investigation can be conducted.

No matter what the data suggest, it is important to
remember that, for anyone suffering from sexual
compulsive behaviors, both the etiology and its related
manifestations are the same: shame and the resulting
sexualized anger. The expression of the behaviors may
differ in males and females. However, the depth of the
afflicted person's wounding and the consequences of
their actions are equally devastating.

Maxine, a tall, striking woman with long, silky blonde
hair, sits in the corner of the room. She is large-breasted,
small-waisted, and wears a hardened smirk on her face.
The room is crowded with six other patients, the primary
therapist, and me. I am running a primary group at The
Meadows. In group, the goal is to help others gain insight
into their behaviors and trauma histories by listening to
the experiences of their peers. Each person will share in
group, with each member giving feedback.

Patients' artwork adorns the fabric walls, along with
large posters delivering reminders of lessons to be learned
in inpatient treatment. The lighting is soft and warm. I
start the group with Maxine's story.

"Are you ready, Maxine?" I ask.

Maxine's hardened expression fades away, replaced by
one that is vulnerable and sad.

"Yeah, I'm ready, but I am a little nervous," she says in
a high-pitched voice that I have to strain to hear.

"That's okay," I say.

Maxine takes a big breath and, when she exhales, she resumes her wary, hardened posture.

"I began drinking in high school," Maxine begins. "And then I started using speed when I moved in with a girlfriend who, of course, was a dealer."

"How old were you?" I ask.

"Sixteen," Maxine says, almost prideful.

"Where were your parents?"

Maxine chuckles as if mocking the question. "My parents were where they always were: traveling, working, or getting stoned." She shrugs her shoulders, off-loading a heavy backpack.

"Living on my own, money was always tight," Maxine continues. "So, to get extra cash, I became an official party girl, which was great, 'cause I also got free drinks," she says, almost as an afterthought.

"What is an 'official party girl'?"

Maxine lights up at the chance to explain. "An official party girl is hired by liquor companies to entertain and wait on men at parties sponsored by the company. We wore short skirts and revealing tops and flirted," she says, pausing to allow a wry smile. "We weren't allowed to have sex or go home with the guys. We could only flirt, you know, have fun."

"How many liquor companies did you do this for?"

"About three."

A common way people hide their sexual anger is through the cognitive distortion called "minimization." Maxine's minimization of being a "party girl" keeps her out of touch with the shame behind her sexualized anger. When Maxine dresses provocatively and flirts at the alcohol-driven parties, she covertly expresses sexual feelings, which she denies in order to avoid feeling the shame that sexuality carries. Maxine's sexualized anger makes her feel powerful and in control, and she does not want to stop. When she complains that men are always hitting on her, sounding like a coy, self-proclaimed victim, she enjoys the pleasure of innocent righteousness.

"What was it like being a party girl?" I ask.

"It was *GREAT*," she gushes, her eyes dancing with blissful reverie.

"But what was really going on? What were you really doing at these parties?" I press. Before I even complete my question, a male patient sitting next to Maxine begins to smirk and nod his head.

"What do you think was going on?" I ask him.

"We call them prick teasers," he says.

Maxine's exuberant mood collapses like a helium balloon deflated by the painful truth of her behavior.

"It's called 'sexualized anger,'" I say with a pause. "My bet is that you were either overtly or covertly sexually traumatized as a child. Is that correct?"

There is a long, thoughtful pause as tears start to form in the corner of Maxine's eyes.

"It was my father," she says through a choked voice. "He always called me his 'sexy lady.'"

"How old were you when he said that?"

"I don't know," she says, pausing to take a mental inventory. "I guess as long as I can remember."

"How did that feel when he said that to you?" I ask.

"It made me feel special, I guess, but it felt kind of gross, too," she says, her voice trailing off.

"And angry?" I ask.

"Yes," she responds. "Yes," she says again, nodding her head. "Angry."

The "chase" is yet another form of acting out through passive-aggressive sexualized anger. When Maxine was a young girl, her father sexually objectified her. Although Maxine craved the attention, it was ultimately traumatizing. In order to get attention from her dad, she discovered she had to be "sexy."

As a little girl, Maxine was clueless as to the meaning of "sexy," but she was desperate and determined to find out. Vigilantly, she watched for clues, and they were not hard to find. Flirting with large-breasted, wasp-waisted women in tight, skimpy clothes was Dad's operating procedure. It became Maxine's sexual template.

As is often the case with sexual addiction, the "high" is not always about having sex. In Maxine's case, it is about the chase, getting attention, and being desirable—and then, as if throwing a bucket of ice-cold water on her admirer, letting him know, "You can't have me!"

Maxine dressed provocatively, flirted, and fished for admiration from men. Her gestures, touches, and seductive display of cleavage sent out the sexual signal that she was available and hungry for sex. But when one of the patrons approached her and asked her for a drink after work, she assumed that he wanted to be sexual. She acted as if she were insulted, even though she had been behaving provocatively. In this scenario, her power lies in her ability to reject him and to imagine in him the shame that, in fact, she feels within herself for having been the illicit object of her own father's sexual objectification. When a patron triggered her traumatic memories of her father, she hid the shame she felt then with the sexualized anger she feels now. When she shoves her shame onto him, she feels that she has been restored. She deludes herself into thinking and feeling that she has resolved the original trauma. This relief is only temporary, and she will inevitably return to that feeling of shame.

Among my clients who have dysfunctional sexuality at the heart of their relationship problems, this passive-aggressive anger hides the truth of their shame core from them. The sense of resentment, shame, rage, and anger that infects their relationships originates in their sense of having lost power and control, even as they were being shamed. Their passive-aggressive manipulations are their way of undoing their disempowerment. They will ruin their attempts at sexual relationship by dysfunctionally trying to win back the power and control that was stolen from them when they were children abused by their primary caregivers.

✧ ✧ ✧ ✧

Lisa sits across from me with a sly smile on her face.

"What's up?" I ask, curious to dig beneath her expression.

"I didn't do my homework again," she says and smiles at me.

"Why not?" I ask.

"Oh . . . I guess I didn't want to."

"Why didn't you want to? What's really going on?"

"I guess I am scared."

"Scared of what?"

"Of having sex."

Sexual withholding is another expression of sexual anger. Lisa has become unwilling to be sexual with her partner because, as a child, she endured sexual abuse. Like others who have suffered such abuse, there is something inside her that will not allow her to be sexual or to give up a part of herself, even though she is willingly in a relationship with someone she loves—and has been in the relationship for years.

As children, abuse victims had to give up themselves and their bodies in order to survive. They are not going to do that again. So the anger at the original perpetrator gets played out in their partnerships. The act of withholding is another way trauma victims create the illusion of power and control. The power and control that was stolen when they were sexually violated is now transferred to their unsuspecting partners.

When Lisa's partner of four years comes to her for sex, every part of her—her emotions, her intellect, and her body—screams. The very innermost part of her being says, "No. I can't give myself again." She may consciously or unconsciously feel that her refusal has put her in control, and she feels some temporary relief. The feeling of control may produce a neurochemical release that produces a high, which paradoxically is also produced by acting out sexually.

"What's so scary?" I ask.

At this question, Lisa begins to cry, "I am so scared, so scared to let go."

"What are you afraid is going to happen?" I ask.

Her tears turn to sobs as she explains.

"I hate sex. I can't have sex. Every time I think of sex, I feel sick to my stomach. I feel like crawling into a little ball and dying. It is not that I don't love my partner or even find him attractive. It's that I am afraid. I am afraid if I have sex, I will lose a part of myself."

"How does your partner feel about your withholding?"

"Oh, I have ways to keep him at bay," she says, her tears subsiding.

"You mean to manipulate him to get what you want?"

"Well, if you want to put it that way," she says, the smirk returning.

It is dawn as the light filters through Lisa's bedroom window. She has been lying awake for several hours, unable to fall back asleep. She has been running the logic over and over in her mind: "I love him. I feel safe with him. I want to be with him. He is a good person, but I can't have sex with him. Will I ever be able to have sex with him? Will I ever be normal? And what is normal?"

Lisa gently shifts her weight, careful not to disturb her partner's slumber. She looks at Ward's face: the slight upturn of his nose; the freckles spotting his cheeks; his plump, rosy lips; and long, dark eyelashes. He looks so peaceful. How can he be the monster poised to steal Lisa's sex?

Lisa feels an internal gash, as if her body and mind are divided like two enemies on a battlefield—her head the logic, her body the terror.

Lisa takes a deep breath, closes her eyes, and flashes on her father and the horror she felt as his hands wandered over her small body. Holding her breath and closing her eyes tightly, she hopes she can erase the horror of her father's touch. In her confusion she wonders: "This is my father; he is supposed to love me, to keep me safe. Am I supposed to feel good about this? Is this his love? If it is, how come I feel so frozen, so scared, so confused, so betrayed?"

"Is it manipulation?" I say, jarring Lisa back to the present.

"Look, call it what you want. I am just protecting myself. It's my body, after all."

"That's true. It is your body. The question is: What do you want to do with your body?"

Lisa is a sexual anorexic, unable to seek or find pleasure in sexual experience. Lisa's sexual template was hammered and forged the day her father violated her through incest. That horrific violation stamped Lisa with the belief that sex equals shame, terror, and powerlessness. Her survival instinct shielded her from that awful shame through passive-aggressive anger, deluding Lisa into feeling that she was in control.

"I feel guilty when I turn my partner down or make excuses for not being sexual," Lisa continues. "But, at the same time, I feel a sense of gratification; it is as if now I have the power."

It is late afternoon as Lisa takes a sip of her coffee. She loves the light this time of day. She has always felt that, right before sunset, time stands still, as if there were a pregnant pause or a long, slow inhalation.

Taking another sip of her coffee, she breathes deeply as if to sustain the magic of the moment. As she fills her lungs, she halts abruptly. Her reverie is interrupted as two lovers cross the street, blocking the fading rays of light.

The woman steals an adoring glance as her partner leans over for a tender kiss. Lisa's stomach tightens. Her breathing is shallow, and she feels disdain rise in her.

"Do I need to see this? Can't they get a room?" she thinks begrudgingly. "Can't they contain themselves?" Lisa feels defiled by what she classifies as a "public display of emotional weakness."

Lisa picks up her coffee and pushes back her metal chair, making a slight squeaking noise. Embarrassed that she may be calling attention to herself, she brushes past the counter of the coffee shop. The lovers, now standing in line, are locked in a loving embrace. Lisa imagines shooting daggers out of her eyes and into their hearts.

The fallout from Lisa's abuse leaves her unable to tolerate any form of sexual energy, whether it is directed at her or not. This public display of physical affection leaves Lisa feeling threatened. To counter her vulnerability, she goes "one-up" and sees the couple as weak, inappropriate, dirty, and disgusting. She thinks, "I can control *my* self; why can't you?" Lisa's sexual template distorts her thinking and emotions so that sex, whether real or imagined, is intolerable and terrifying.

"So, doing your homework would mean what?" I ask.

"It would mean that I might get better."

"And what's wrong with that?"

"I like it where I am. It feels safe," Lisa says.

Shortly after this session, Lisa failed to return to therapy. Her demons, at least for now, had won. Her feelings of terror outweighed her hope for a new freedom, a freedom from the prison her father had locked her in so many years ago.

Unlike passive-aggressive sexual anger, aggressive behavior is direct and may include intimidation, threats, and physical and emotional aggression. Rape, sexual incest, and molestation are the most extreme expressions of sexual anger. These extreme violations, however, are more the exception than the rule for most sexually compulsive individuals. For most sexual addicts, aggressive sexual anger, masked by the sexual objectification of self or others, serves to divert painful awareness from the objectifier's shame.

Take, for example, Max, who pursues an inappropriate sexual relationship with a subordinate at work. Or Jill, who becomes a dominatrix so that she can role-play torture or degradation of herself and her tricks. Or Milton, who spends hours each day downloading pornography onto his computer and masturbating. All of these are overt aggressive behaviors that attempt to mitigate shame and pain.

A more convoluted manner of mitigating shame and pain combines passive-aggressive anger with aggressive anger.

As the plane begins its descent, the lights of the city break through the cloud cover. To Andy, the city looks like a magical kingdom, its twinkling lights like jewels beckoning him to come and play. The city is a place of mystery and adventure, such a contrast from Andy's life in Boston. Married to a wife whom he perceives as boring, Andy lives a life of monotonous drudgery.

Loosening his tie, he imagines what the next few days will bring. An accountant by trade, Andy has secured several accounts that afford him frequent trips into the city.

As the plane continues its descent, Andy feels his old self shedding like a snakeskin. The tension from the day begins to unwind, and his mind keenly focuses as euphoria spreads throughout his body.

As we have pointed out, anger is a way for sex addicts to feel in control and, when addicts act in both a passive-aggressive and an aggressive manner, their lives become double-edged swords. The passive side allows for a secret life of lies, betrayal, and intrigue that, fragment by precious fragment, steals trust from partners, bosses, children, friends, and family, until the addict's lies and betrayals are exposed. The aggressive side builds and builds until it heedlessly takes what it wants, with little or no regard for consequences, either moral or physical.

Andy climbs the steps outside the church. His seven-year-old legs have to stretch like a track star hurdling each gate. Holding his father's hand provides physical stability. However, his emotional state is as fragile as Belleek china.

Andy's mother died three days ago. She had been the center of his world. A car crash stole her away.

Dizzy from the day's activities and shocked by the reality of his life, Andy feels bewildered and lost. Lying on the window seat, he watches the black-clad mourners mingling in the living room. Closing his eyes and drifting off to sleep, he feels a gentle touch. In his groggy state, he thinks of his mother, her loving and comforting nature. He wants to stay, drifting in the comfort of her memory, but he is jolted out of his haze by his father's voice.

"Son, Grandma and Aunt Kate want to talk to you, so sit up and listen up, okay?" his father says, more like a coach sending out his star quarterback than a dad comforting a son's loss.

Andy sits up to face what feels like a firing squad: His grandmother and aunt, both difficult and demanding women, are crouched over him like a double-barreled shotgun ready to explode.

"Andy, you have to be strong," they begin.

"Your dad has been through an awful shock, and you need to help by being his right-hand man. You know he travels a lot, and you will need to help with your younger sister. You'll need to be the man around the house while he is gone. Do you think you can do that?" they ask with a pause that hangs in the air.

Andy's family's reaction to grief involves a no-talk, no-feel rule, which demands that Andy stuff his feelings. He will be shaped into a robotic caretaker who simmers with resentment and anger.

As Andy stumbles down the hall to the bathroom, he can hear voices from his parents' room. At first, Andy's heart leaps, as he believes he hears his mother's voice. Pushing open the half-closed door, Andy is jarred awake by seeing Aunt Kate entwined in his father's arms, laughing and giggling. Abruptly they stop, hearing the creak of the door.

"Go back to bed, son," Andy's father bellows from the bed. "GO!" he calls out in a firmer and more panicked tone.

Andy has suffered an earth-shattering betrayal that will haunt him and his relationship with women for the rest of his life. His mother's death, although an accident, will crush his ability to trust women. Aunt Kate's behavior will teach Andy the sordid dynamic of triangulation, a web of lies and secrets between three people, which will cement the cornerstone of Andy's sexual addiction.

Andy, unhappy in his marriage but afraid to leave his wife, has aggressively pursued what he believes is a "relationship" with a prostitute named Angel.

"She is in love with me," Andy says with conviction.

"Umm . . . really?" I reply.

"Yes, she *IS,*" he says, emphasizing the "is" as if that will help convince me of the validity of his delusional fantasy.

Andy is in therapy because his wife has given him an ultimatum, not because he wants to give up Angel. Either he becomes emotionally available and spends more time with her and the boys, or she files for divorce.

Andy sits slumped on the couch, his suit wrinkled, his glasses tilted off-center, looking as if he has just rolled out of bed. Andy is a boiling pot of resentments and repressed anger. He feels trapped in his marriage and pretends to love a woman for whom he feels only obligation. Andy has little desire to change his avoidant behaviors.

"So tell me, Andy, does your wife know that you keep a prostitute stashed in Manhattan?" I ask.

"No," he says in a tone indicating how stupid it would be to blow his cover.

"How do you think she would feel if she really knew what you were doing on your business trips?"

"You know what?" he says, somewhat annoyed. "My wife is a great lady. I need to spend more time with her and the kids. I know that, and I'm going to start doing that; I have to. But New York is mine. I work hard, and the fact is, I deserve it."

Andy has spent extensive time, money, and energy on his secret life—keeping Angel in an expensive apartment, showering her with gifts, taking her out for expensive meals, and, of course, having unlimited and unrestrained sexual encounters.

"I already started making it up to my wife," Andy says like a kid seeking approval.

"How so?" I ask.

"I took her with me to New York last week. We stayed at The Plaza, went shopping, saw a play... you know, did it up right."

"And what about Angel? Did you see her?" I ask.

The theater lobby is mobbed. Andy practically had to sell his soul to get tickets to opening night. Stopping at the bar, Andy throws back a stiff one while his wife stands mesmerized by the crowd. Grabbing his wife's elbow, he steers her through the crowd to their seats.

"So did you contact Angel?" I ask again.

"Sort of," he says.

As the lights dim, the familiar perfume wafts to Andy's nostrils. Looking past his wife, he steals a brief glance, noticing Angel's silky black hair and low-cut dress. Seated next to his wife, Angel adjusts her view as the curtain slowly rises. Andy, who had bought her a seat, feels the euphoria and a feeling of profound satisfaction.

Andy has concocted what, for him, is the most extremely dangerous and powerful sexual challenge. Like the little boy who had no control, he has deluded himself into believing that he is in control of both his wife and his prostitute, who are the unconscious substitutes for his original abusers: his mother and his aunt. He can win the whole sexual jackpot. In fact, he has set himself up to crash, burn, and lose everything. Both women will recognize him for the out-of-control liar he has become. He has doomed himself to suffer the loss and shame that he believes subconsciously are appropriate for someone as worthless and undeserving as he is.

Chapter 6

ACTING OUT AND ACTING IN: THE SOCIALLY FORGIVABLE BEHAVIORS

The ways in which sexually dysfunctional individuals display their pathology are varied, ranging from voyeurism to cross-dressing, cybersex to sexual anorexia (i.e., aversion to sex), sadomasochism to all points between. Not only do specific behaviors vary, there is usually more than one traumatic template behind the presenting symptoms.

It is important for me, in observing my patients and listening to their histories, to recognize certain points in their family histories when their primary caregivers inflicted the original wounds that formed their trauma. The harsh judgment that society passes on many addicts' behaviors, viewing them as perverse, cruel, or weird, is unfair. They are the inevitable products of childhood wounding.

Trauma creates a compulsion to repeat the traumatic moment whenever its memory is stirred by later events. Trauma freezes us in the ego-state of when we were first traumatized. This freezing in time is often called "arrested development."

To uncloak the mystery that hides this moment is crucial. It's a first step in reducing an individual's shame to a level low enough that they can begin to believe they are worthy of respect and capable of recovery. For the sake of tracking these crucial moments, let's look at some sexually dysfunctional behaviors planted in the poisoned soil of childhood abuse.

Cybersex

Before we get into the specifics of behaviors, let's look at the behaviors sheltered under the cybersex umbrella. When cybersex first came on the scene, we dubbed it "the crack cocaine of sex addiction" because of its accessibility and affordability. The Internet allowed for a quick progression of the disease; if addicts hadn't been acting out at all, or hadn't progressed in their behaviors, the Internet instantly provided the inflammatory spark.

Addicts could now access their secret sex world by pushing a button. They no longer had to cruise the streets, go to seedy adult bookstores, or put themselves at physical risk. They could find whatever they craved any time of the day or night, right from the comfort of their homes.

Over $1 billion is made annually by the cybersex industry as a whole (meaning any site containing sexual content). The business is expected to grow by $5 to $7 billion over the next five years.

It was not just men who were acting out; 32 million women visited at least one pornography website in one month of 2004 alone.

In addition, 41 percent of women said they had deliberately viewed or downloaded pornographic pictures and movies. However, women primarily act out in chat rooms—a breeding ground for intrigue, seduction, and fantasy.

For me, the most shocking statistic is that the largest group of viewers of Internet porn is children ages 12 to 17. Even more devastating are the statistics related to child pornography:

- Approximately 20 percent of all Internet pornography involves children.
- Child pornography has become a $3 billion annual industry.
- According to the National Center for Missing and Exploited Children (NCMEC), child pornography reports increased 39 percent in 2004. Ernie Allen, president and CEO of NCMEC, states that the statistics show a significant and steady increase in child pornography reports.
- More than 20,000 images of child pornography are posted on the Internet every week.

Not only are the statistics hard to grasp, but so is the advancement of technology. It is now possible to set up virtual worlds of sexual contact using remote devices that can be stimulated from different locations by different people. The receiver merely attaches a device to his genitals, and his partner uses a keypad to control the levels of stimulation. Cell phones, web cams, and Blackberries all can be integrated into the addict's world to enhance the acting-out experience.

All aspects of the addiction cycle are applicable to online behaviors, as are the needs for power and control. You can be anything, say anything, request anything, and never risk exposure. By the click of a button, you are gone, in a new space, seducing and exploring—getting high.

Cybersex is especially appealing to those who dissociate because it creates an immediate escape into a fantasy world. Cybersex is also alluring for the shame-based client because of the low risk of emotional rejection.

For those who fuse sex with intensity, running multiple programs simultaneously amplifies their high. They can participate in chat rooms, download pornography, instant message, and send sexual images of themselves via web cam, all at the same time.

With the advent of cybersex, the repercussions for sex addicts have been devastating. One of the biggest issues for sexual addicts is impulse control, and the Internet allows the addict's gratification—"I want what I want when I want it"—to be instant.

No matter how the addict acts out, he can find it in the world of cybersex—a world that continues to expand at lightning speed.

Paying for Sex

Clients who pay for sex (this includes street prostitutes, call-up escort services, massage parlors, and strip clubs, as well as Internet porn sites) often do not see their acting out as dysfunctional; rather, they see it as self-nurturing.

I believe that these clients were abandoned by their primary caregivers and never developed the capacity for complex intimacy in a relationship. The sexual element in their sex-for-hire escapades is not as strong as their desire for connection and intimacy.

The details of the sexual liaison are distorted re-creations of the parental intimacy they deserved, yearned for, and never got. These johns seek out sex partners who remind them of their abusers, seeking to undo the lack of control they had over their caregivers—with a cash contract taking the place of unconditional parental love.

It does not matter whether the initial wounding was perpetrated by mother, father, babysitter, nanny, or next-door neighbor. The victim will look for someone with a resemblance to that person. Whenever I have a client who pays for sex, I want to know specifically the details involved in their acting-out activities: how the sex partner looks, sounds, and smells. Like a detective with forensic evidence, I trace a path back to the identity and modus operandi of the original abuser.

Let's go back to Ben, whom we got to know in Chapter 5, first abandoned by his mother and then by Nanny. Ben is a classic example of how, through a wounding of abandonment and shame, a person becomes addicted to the world of sex for hire. Desperate for love and attention, Ben developed an "attachment disorder," which occurs when a child is unable to bond with his primary caregivers. An attachment disorder takes place

when the primary caregiver cannot provide emotional
and physical nurturing for her child. The causes can
include:

- Mental illness
- Physical illness
- Disabilities
- Addictions
- Depression
- Inadequate parenting skills
- Frequent moves
- A temperament not matching the child's
- Death
- Divorce

Ben looks around the dark room in terror. From the
inside of his crib, he cannot see anything but the wooden
slats in his tiny world. He can hear his parents breathing,
but he cannot move or twist himself around to see them
sleeping in the bed next to him.

Ben is swaddled so tightly in his blanket, each breath
becomes a gasp. Ben, an asthmatic baby, lies terrified and
frantic for comfort and attention. His cries are
unanswered as he desperately struggles to catch his next
breath.

"I can remember everything," Ben says, squinting his
eye as if he is watching a movie in his head.

"You were very young," I say.

"Yes, I was an infant, but I remember it all."

"It must have been terrifying," I respond, imagining

the impact of his abuse.

"It was."

"Do you know why she did not pick you up or care for you?"

"I have asked her, and she said the doctor told her to let me cry."

The primal struggle that Ben repeatedly endured left him with a preverbal wound so deep it arrested his normal emotional development. As we have discussed, the earlier the wounding, or the earlier the brain receives messages that it needs to operate in survival mode, the more severe is the impact on the child's emotional development.

...According to Michael Common and Patrice Miller's research at the Harvard Department of Psychiatry, the early stress from separation of a primary caregiver causes changes in the infant's brain and can alter the development of an infant's mind, making him abnormally susceptible to stress in his adult life. They write: "Parents should realize that having their babies cry unnecessarily harms the baby permanently. It changes the nervous system so they're overly sensitive to future trauma."[3]

This was the case for Ben, whose primal core belief impaired his ability to trust or feel safe. He was often on

[3]Children Need Touching and Attention, Harvard Researchers Say," Alvin Powell, *Harvard University Gazette*, April 09, 1998

the edge of frantic anxiety attacks, which he learned to soothe through his sexual acting-out addiction.

In the massage parlor, Ben would talk intimately with the large-breasted, dark-skinned prostitutes and ask to lie next to them so that he could rest his head on their breasts. Having had no power or control over his mother's abuse or his wife's distracted attention after the birth of twins, Ben purchased power and control with money. He paid for the assurance that he would not be rejected. But the cash bargain came with terrible shame. He would continue to feel shame until he could give it back to the person to whom it belonged: the mother who would not listen to his need for her love and attention when he was a baby.

Because of Ben's severe neglect, he never developed the capacity for complex intimacy in a relationship. The sexual element in his sex-for-hire escapades is not as strong as his desire for connection and intimacy.

The details of the sexual liaison are distorted re-creations of the parental intimacy he deserved, yearned for, and never got. Ben sought out sex partners who remind him of his abusers and sought to undo the lack of control he had over his caregivers, with a cash contract taking the place of unconditional parental love.

Seductive Role Sex

For women, seductive role sex often does not have as its end goal sexual intercourse. The woman flirts and seduces, puffing herself up with a sense of control, power, and allure. But once she has seduced the object of her attentions, she cuts him off, sublimating her anger and rage. If she knew why she was so angry, she would not feel so powerful. She would probably feel like the powerless child who is still driving her adult behavior.

The seducer who is overtly looking to force herself into a sexual relationship is ultimately frightened of the consequences. She believes that, if she gives a man sex, he will leave her. She will lose control and power. The paradox is lost on her.

What lies behind the anger and rage is the fear of being abandoned. But why do these women seduce in the first place, if they are frightened that the consequence of seduction is abandonment?

Such an individual may have had a father who was emotionally unavailable or who sexually acted out with women whom he used and tossed away. The daughter tries to seduce her negligent father into intimacy, but she fails. To further her cause with him, she will examine his taste in women to see what attracts him. She sees that he's attracted to sexually seductive women, and she sees that he abandons them.

So she is caught in a bind. When she wants a man, she thinks she must be seductive. When she gets the man in her clutches, she must flee from him in order not to be abandoned.

The dysfunctionality of this emotional Catch-22 is blatant, but the seductive woman often deludes herself into believing that because "she can get anyone she wants," she is in control and is powerful and desirable. She fails to recognize that her sexual seductiveness leaves her not only sexually unsatisfied, but filled with shame and fear.

Let's recall the story of Maxine, who, as an "official party girl," found sexual power and control. Maxine's father, a successful trial lawyer, was Maxine's hero. Smart, articulate, charming, attractive, and commanding, he seemed to be the center of whatever world he entered.

Everything Maxine achieved, she did for her father's approval. A straight-A student, captain of the basketball team, and homecoming queen, she was fueled by an unrelenting drive to be perfect.

It was hard for Maxine to fall asleep, despite the late hour. She could hear the party below, from which she had been dismissed several hours ago.

There were heavy drinking and drug use, naked people in the hot tub, whipped cream being licked off of women's breasts. Her father was the ringleader of it all.

"Where was your mother during these parties?" I ask.

"She was there with everybody else," Maxine says matter-of-factly.

"She was participating?"

"Yes. My parents were unofficial swingers."

"What do you mean, 'unofficial'?"

"Well, they never went to clubs or anything like that—at least I never knew about it—but they had an open marriage for a while."

Maxine creeps down the staircase to get a better look. A stripper has arrived, an obvious birthday present for her father, and she has climbed on top of the dining-room table.

"My dad was mesmerized," Maxine says. "He was positioned so I could see the expression on his face. He looked like he was whooping it up, like all the rest of them."

"How did you feel, watching his response?" I ask.

"I was shocked. I mean, she wasn't that good of a dancer or that attractive, so I was surprised he was so into it."

Maxine hears the thunder as she pulls out her dress-up clothes. The rain is beating on the picture windows as she makes her way down the stairway. She joins her father, who is nursing his hangover in the den. He lets out a low moan as the opposing team scores another touchdown. "What the hell?" he yells, holding his throbbing head.

Maxine, absorbed in her production, positions herself in front of the TV.

"Watch me, Daddy," Maxine says, as she spins and gyrates, throwing off her pink boa.

Her father strains to see the replay of the game between her frantic movements. "Oh, sweetie, you are one sexy lady," his says distractedly.

Maxine continues dancing, as her father, more attentive when the commercial begins, starts to laugh.

"Maxine, where'd you learn to be so sexy? Come here. You're Daddy's princess, aren't you?" For a fleeting moment, Maxine feels like a star. She feels as if the heavens have shone a spotlight on the two of them.

Running into her father's arms, she squeezes him with all her might. "Okay, okay, sweetie, now Daddy needs to see what's happening with the game," he says, and pushes her off his lap.

Maxine's father was emotionally unavailable. Instead of being there for Maxine, he acted out sexually in drunken and drugged stupors.

In our culture, women tend to be flirty and needy, offering full surrender, whereas men tend to be caretakers, seductively generous from the one-up stance, while, at the same time, keeping their distance. That is because, in our culture, most women have been emotionally disempowered and feel they need a man to take care of them on an emotional level. They develop passive-aggressive techniques to get what they want by appearing vulnerable. They flaunt their neediness as a seduction technique. Because, in our culture, men have been falsely empowered to think that they need to take care of needy women, it feeds their grandiosity to give until they get bored.

Both the love avoidant, who avoids intimacy through grandiose caretaking, and the love addict, who avoids intimacy through neediness, use sex to manipulate their partners in order to compensate for their own emotional delinquencies. Each feels a painful lack of self-esteem. Because our self-esteem cannot be given to us from the outside, manipulating our partners so that their love will make us whole is not only a fruitless task, but is evidence of our childhood wounding.

"What I learned from my father," Maxine says with sadness in her voice, "was to abandon myself. I wanted him so much. I ached for his attention, and where did it get me?" she says with tears flowing down her face. "A bunch of sick relationships, with a bunch of sick men, all of whom could give a shit about me . . . every last one of them, just like my father."

"So what do you need to do now?" I ask.

Maxine looks at me blankly, her eyes red and swollen,

her body rolled onto the couch, clutching the pillow in a near-fetal position. "I need," she says in a childlike tone, "someone to love me." Her tears continue to flow.

In successful therapy, the avoidant and the addict will discover that the wound from which they both suffer is abandonment. Neither got the kind of parenting that supported belief in his or her authentic humanity. They were taught that they needed something other than what they were. The avoidant was taught to feel less than (needy), the addict taught to feel more than (grandiose). Both feelings are lies that have made inevitable the confusion of self-esteem with one-down or one-up manipulation.

"Do you think you can love yourself?" I ask Maxine.

"Good God," Maxine says, sitting up. "That's what it all comes down to, doesn't it?" she says with some resolve.

"Yes, it does, unless you want to live in the constant shadow of your father's abuse."

"Well, I've done that for long enough, and look where it has gotten me," she says.

"Yes, and look at where you could go from here," I say.

"Yeah," Maxine says with a quick smile, her body more relaxed. "Look where I can go from here." Her smile widens. "To a lot better place than where I've been."

Fantasy Sex

Fantasy sex is one of the most powerful and challenging behaviors to treat because the addict has created a 24/7 IV drip. Whenever the addict wants to escape or get high, he opens the drip and there is instant relief. When I am training therapists, I ask them to think of their favorite food. Chocolate is often their answer. I ask them to think of the specific type of chocolate: dark, milk, bittersweet, etc., then to imagine opening the package, the sound of the crinkle of the paper, the first whiff of the aroma, snapping off the first piece, placing it in their mouths, experiencing the texture and the taste.

They are now in a chemically altered trance state. The detailed sensuous recall of the chocolate bar has induced the chemicals in the brain that create a high. This is similar to what happens for a fantasy addict when he imagines his sexual vignettes.

Often the fantasy addict has had one particular fantasy, or theme of the fantasy, that has been with them since the fantasy began: He is rescued, he is in control, he is in physical pain, he is desired. The fantasy can vary. However, the same fantasy, or slight variations on the theme, can be with addicts their entire lives.

It is a crisp fall day as Barbara shuffles through the dry oak leaves that lie like a carpet in the field behind her apartment. The heavily wooded lot has become Barbara's escape, a sanctuary for her imaginary world.

An only child to a single mom, Barbara is starved for attention. Her mother, who holds down two jobs to make ends meet, is exhausted on weekends and has little time to spend with Barbara. Barbara knows nothing about her biological father—only that "he was a bad mistake and a distant memory."

Her cousins who live down the street, eight years older

than six-year-old Barbara, often taunt and tease her, calling her "Bastard Barbara." She is often sent there to spend the night when her mother works late.

Barbara fights off the loneliness and shame that stalk her by escaping into her mind. In her fantasies, Barbara is never alone: She is the object of desire, a treasured princess. The tall, dark trees come alive; they are her admirers, her lovers.

In this fantasy, Barbara is in control; she has the power. No longer a victim, she is the desired object, and she mainlines the euphoric drip of her imagined world.

Barbara, a petite, freckled redhead whose voice is surprisingly commanding, has come into treatment to examine her unsuccessful relationships.

"Did your fantasies have a theme?" I ask.

"Yeah, they did," she says. "I was always hurt; usually I was in a car accident, and some handsome paramedic would rescue me. The minute our eyes met, we were in love. Our encounter would lead to passionate lovemaking."

"How long did your fantasy last?" I ask.

"For years."

"Did the fantasy ever deviate?"

"Only in small details. In the winter, when it was too cold to go outside, I would play in the basement. Down there were these columns that supported the building, and I substituted the columns for the trees. When I went to school, I would do the same thing in the orchard next to the playground."

"You wouldn't play with other kids?" I ask.

"Not usually. I liked my fantasy world. I spent so much time in it, I had a hard time relating to other kids."

This kind of reliance on fantasy is a form of dissociation trauma, which enables the victim to separate from the reality of what she is feeling. Barbara had found an escape from her desperate need for love and attention. In her mind, she was desired, she was loved, and, most important, she had control.

"What did it feel like when you went into your fantasy?" I ask.

"It was like slow molasses pouring over me—a sweet, luxurious euphoria that made all the pain go away."

"How long did this fantasy last?"

"Until I came in here for treatment," she says matter-of-factly.

For fantasy addicts, fantasy becomes part of their identity, a reflex as automatic as breathing. The dependence on this escape can become so severe that the idea of giving it up feels like the death of an old intimate friend. Often the withdrawal that fantasy addicts face is extreme because of the immediate loss of the chemicals induced by the chemically-altered brain. Living in the "here and now" immediately releases an overwhelming flood of feelings. The fantasy addict feels disoriented, overwhelmed, and desperate to escape back into familiar fantasy, where he feels he has control.

"How do you think your fantasy world has affected your relationships?" I ask.

Barbara lets out a spontaneous laugh, which surprises even her.

"Everything outside my fantasy world is so boring. I love that I can create whatever I want, in whatever scenario I want, whenever I want. Riding the train home from work, changing my son's diapers, having sex with my boyfriend. . . . My fantasies are always more exciting than my everyday life."

"So it is the desire for intensity that the fantasy creates."

"Yes, and the fact that nothing or no one can live up to my fantasy world. I am always in control."

"So it's that need to be in control, to have all the attention, to feel special, that makes it hard to let go?"

"Yes," Barbara says as tears flow down her cheeks.

Relational intimacy, both emotional and physical, will not be possible for Barbara until she lets go of her drug and grieves her traumatic childhood. Like all addicts, she needs to become present in the here and now, allowing the intensity of her private world to fade away.

Acting In

With all addictive behaviors, there is a cycle or pattern that is predictable and ritualized. For the healing process to begin, it is paramount for the individual to understand and intervene in this cycle.

As addicts, we have learned to live in extremes: extreme behavior, extreme thoughts, and extreme feelings. We live this way because unconsciously we are attempting to gain control or achieve moderation. It is much like a pendulum that swings from one side to the other, never stopping or finding a sense of balance or moderation.

This is the life of a sex addict, a roller coaster life of emotional imbalance. The goal of treatment and sexual health is learning to live a moderate, balanced life.

Those who "act out" express their sexualized anger overtly. Those who "act in" suppress their sexualized anger. As in the acting-out cycle, the acting-in cycle is motivated by the desire to gain power and control over traumatic memories, in order to avoid the loss of control, fear, and shame that the memories provoke.

When those who act in are provoked by memories of their original wounding, they become obsessed with strategies to protect against losing control over their bodies. These strategies distance them from sexual involvement. They can become so preoccupied with keeping their sexual distance that they become hypervigilant, fearful, and almost panicky.

They develop distancing strategies such as coming home late from work so that they do not have to face their spouses. At the sign of any sexual signals from their partners, they may pick a fight. When it is time to go to bed, they may make up a project that demands their attention or find a book that is too engrossing to put down. They may get too drunk for sex.

They sometimes make themselves physically unattractive by dressing badly. Men will not shave; women will not wear makeup. They do not bathe or use deodorant. They wear their unattractiveness like body armor.

It is a sad irony that those who act in take pride in these sexual deprivations. They are in denial that their distancing and self-abnegation are founded on a basis of shame. So, instead of feeling one-down, they go one-up by convincing themselves that they have developed an admirable discipline that makes them superior to the loose, immoral, irresponsible sexual indulgences of those who act out. They are like food addicts who can constrain themselves from eating but think that all fat people are disgusting. Their one-upsmanship is really a projection of their own low self-esteem around the fear of losing sexual control.

Acting in and acting out can alternate with one another. A client may tell me that he doesn't act out for six months, but then he binges on cocaine and pays a dozen prostitutes in a weekend. These extreme swings dysfunctionally provide addicts with the feeling that they are in control of their excesses, and they prove it by their temporary returns to deprivation. Whether in the binge or deprivation side of the cycle, they have the illusion of being in control when in reality they are out of control. Moderation, an essential part of a healthy emotional life, is beyond them.

Acting-out individuals are subject to long periods when they alternate between acting out and false recovery, which is acting in masquerading as recovery. After a period of destructive acting out, individuals will come to a recovery facility and accept a celibacy contract. After treatment, they rigidly adhere to sexual deprivation and do not have sex for possibly three years. In another scenario, a woman divorces from a marriage in which both partners had been sexually acting out. For the next five years, she has no sex. Now, instead of acting out, she is acting in. The goal in recovery is to be moderate, to learn to live neither in excess nor in deprivation.

This cycle of acting out alternating with acting in characterizes many dysfunctional relationships between husband and wife or other committed partners. Usually one is a love addict and the other a love avoidant. A lot of people enter relationships thinking that sex equals love. Love addicts think that sex will prove that they are worthwhile. Love avoidants think that, by providing sex, they are doing their caretaking duty, which their immature, needy parents taught them was the meaning of love.

When they find that they are miserable despite the sex, their fantasies about love and sex are shattered. The love addict acts in and shuts down sexually. Her knight in shining armor has failed her. The other partner, the love avoidant, resents this deprivation and now has an excuse to get sex outside the painful relationship. It's what he really wanted to do anyway. He hates being dutiful.

The acting-out partner has probably unconsciously picked the acting-in partner because, as a love avoidant, he considers love a painful duty, and he senses how desperately his partner needs love. Fulfilling this desperate need gives him the power upon which his self-importance rests. Now, when the pain of deprivation is manifested, he can do what he always wanted to do: act out sexually with no relationship obligations. He develops a resentment that his partner is not available to him, and he believes he is fully justified in getting what he wants outside the relationship.

If both partners are acting in, the relationship can go on forever. I do not see a lot of acting-in couples in treatment. They seem happy, and their dysfunctional emotions are well hidden. They have grown very familiar with their acting-in behavior, and they think it is normal. The calm is shattered when they get into a relationship with someone who demands that they be sexual and emotionally vulnerable. Then they realize that they really do have a problem.

When both partners are acting out sexually, chaos often ensues. One method of controlling the sexual chaos is by trying to normalize it, making it part of an accepted routine. This is common with people who go to swingers' clubs. They tell themselves that the club is as normal as a bingo game or a night at the movies. They tell each other that it is fun and exciting. They engage in threesomes and role-play dress-up.

Acting out can become intense and life-consuming as it becomes the basis of what a couple thinks their relationship is all about. Often both partners are acting out outside of the primary relationship, sometimes with the permission of their partners. This can seem comfortable and in control until someone gets arrested, gets a disease, or is publicly condemned. Then there is a crisis.

In the middle of these mutual acting-out cycles, one of the partners may swing into acting in. If the acting-out partner gets caught, he might swing over to the acting-in side. Or I have known of acting-in people who have found out that their partners are having multiple affairs and then, in resentment, act out. It is not necessarily their propensity, but their form of retaliation. When their acting-out partners discover that they are being "betrayed," they are devastated and may choose sexual deprivation, swinging back to acting in.

Chapter 7

ACTING OUT: THE LESS UNDERSTOOD AND SOCIALLY UNFORGIVABLE BEHAVIORS

As a culture, we tend to stigmatize certain sexual acts or behaviors. If a person's sexual templates and related behaviors lie in the less understood, acceptable, or unforgivable realms, recovery can prove even more of a challenge. The associated shame makes it that much more difficult to own, talk about, treat, or heal. I am not saying that we should condone such behavior, but that we should educate ourselves about the compulsions that generate it.

Voyeuristic Sex

Voyeurs are aroused through visual stimulation, and voyeurism is a passive-aggressive acting-out behavior. This kind of passivity-cloaking aggression originates at the time of the original childhood wounding, when the child's angry reaction to abuse needed to be camouflaged so as not to invite further abuse. Passive-aggression is a common trait in most acting-out sexual behaviors, because such behaviors seek to replicate the conditions under which the original wounding took place—with one crucial change: The victim of the original abuse becomes the perpetrator. He seeks the power and control he did not have as a child, which, he delusionally believes, will bring him pleasure and safety.

Although the voyeur is passively distancing himself from any intimate contact, he is, at the same time, unilaterally and aggressively appropriating a sexual privilege. The culmination of the peeping may be in orgasm achieved during the watching, or the orgasm can be delayed until the voyeur, having stored up his images, masturbates in privacy. When the pleasure is delayed and played out with stored images or euphoric recall, the template behind it reflects an early childhood adaptation to fantasy. This will lead to a search for the origins of such an adaptation in childhood.

It is mid-August, and the air hangs like thick velvet curtains. These are the dog days of summer, but Jake, who sits on the curb outside his four-story row house, is oblivious to the humidity. He is buried deep in his imagined world, dragging his stick across the sewer grate, magically transforming it into banjo strings, like the banjo his father plays on weekends in the pub on the corner.

"Hey, Jakey," his friends yell from down the street.

Jake, jolted out of his imagined world, attempts to intercept the softball flying by his head.

"Got ya," they tauntingly jeer, cracking themselves up

with laughter.

"You're such a pussy," the ringleader says.

Jake, who has taught himself not to react to the jabs, picks up the ball and tosses it back.

"Where's the stick?" another boy asks.

Jake averts his eyes in self-reproach. "Forgot it," he says and turns to climb up the stoop to his tenement.

"Wait here, guys," Jake says over his shoulder, but the boys, right on his tail, follow Jake into the dark, dingy foyer.

"Who's there?" his mother calls out.

"Just me, Ma," Jake says, knowing she is on one of her afternoon binges.

Turning the corner to enter the living room, Jake stops, and the boys run into each other.

"Shit," Jake mutters under his breath.

"What? What are you doing?" Jake's mother asks, slightly raising her head and then letting it fall.

Spread out in only panties and bra, his mother says in a slurred voice, "Oh, hey, boys; come on in," as she waves her extended arm.

The boys quickly turn away in fear and disgust. "We'll meet you outside," one of the boys says, slamming the screen door.

Jake's mother's shameless behavior has been a constant throughout his ten years of life. An alcoholic like her husband, she has often passed out by mid-afternoon, lying naked or half-clad in an open robe or a revealing nightgown.

Jake is torn about his feelings for his mother. When his

mother, still a beauty, is sober, she is loving and attentive, but these times are few and far between. More often, she is a sloppy, abusive, neglectful drunk, and that's what Jake has come to expect from her.

Jake blinks at the bright sunlight as he steps out onto the stoop. He hears the boys' snickers as he leaps down to the sidewalk. "Let's go," he yells, attempting to deflect humiliating taunts and putdowns. Jake, already adept at emotional survival, has learned to manipulate situations to avoid feelings of shame. Jake stuffs those feelings deep down into the cavern of his core, where they will eventually morph into the anger that fuels his secret life.

Jake's experiences with his mother's abusive behavior are the nucleus for his sexual template. The anger, shame, fear, arousal, excitement, and curiosity all fuse in a confusing and overwhelming configuration that fuels his compulsive sexual behavior.

Jake, like all voyeurs, is aroused through visual stimulation. Because of the physical distance and anonymity from which it is committed, voyeurism is a passive-aggressive acting-out behavior. The victim does not know he or she is being violated. This kind of passivity-cloaking aggression has its origins in the original childhood wounding, when the child's shame reaction to abuse needs to be camouflaged so as not to invite further abuse or even ostracism.

As we have already discussed, passive aggression is a common trait in most acting-out sexual behaviors, because such behaviors seek to replicate the conditions under which the original wounding took place—but with one crucial change: The victim of the original abuse becomes the perpetrator. He seeks the power and control he did not have as a child. It becomes his unconscious motivation to repeat the behaviors that were perpetrated for resolution and a feeling of safety.

Jake is awakened by a low moaning sound, which turns to shortened gasps for air. Afraid and confused, he allows the glare of the streetlights to guide him down the hallway. The noise changes again into deep guttural sounds, as if someone is being hurt or tortured. Tiptoeing to the threshold of his parents' room, Jake is riveted by the outline of his mother's body, entwined with a man who is not his father. Jake's confusion merges with curiosity as he watches his mother writhe and moan.

Intuitively Jake knows this is not meant for him to see. This forbidden voyeurism is immediately seared into his memory, creating a disturbing clash of emotions. On one hand is Jake's desire to worship his mother. On the other, he retains a picture of her as a sexual outlaw who inculcated him with shame in the face of sexual pleasure. This pleasure is fused to the danger of having spied on her, risking exposure.

This powerful forbidden experience is among Jake's first intimate sexual memories, and it will traumatize him.

A heterosexual boy who sees a naked woman is going to be aroused, but there's a problem when she is his mother. It is pleasurable, but it is bad. It is pleasurable, but it is secretive. It is pleasurable, but it is shameful. When Jake seeks sexual gratification, the sex will have to be secretive, bad, shameful, and as intense as incest.

The high for voyeurs is hardly ever the orgasm itself. The high is what surrounds it—what re-creates that original trauma: the danger, secrecy, and risk of being caught. That is when Jake feels safe and comfortable, back with Mother. But this time, it is okay—except for the inevitable shame, which is killing him emotionally.

Jake sits in my office, still resembling the gawky child he has described to me. Only twenty-five, Jake has been arrested three times for the passive, violent act of voyeurism. The court has ordered him into treatment, and he is eager to get help.

"I want to stop," Jake says with conviction.

"Then you can," I say. "That's the first step to change: the willingness."

"Well, I am willing."

Like many compulsive people, sex addicts craft their lives to fit their addictions, and Jake is no exception.

"They have a really hot band at the hotel, so tonight is going to be a wild one," Jake's manager says to the parking-lot attendants where Jake works. "I want everybody on their toes. So let's roll," his boss says, clapping his hands.

The headlights of the cars heading for the rock concert cut through the darkness as Jake readies himself to open his first car door. As the car slides to a stop, Jake reaches for the doorknob, his heart beating fast and blood pumping through his veins as if he were in the middle of a boxing match.

"So in college you were a parking-lot valet?" I ask.

"Um hmm," Jake says, nodding his head.

"Tell me how you acted out in this situation."

Jake knew these hot, balmy nights brought the best possible odds. Long, tan legs slid open as they exited the cars in short skirts. Jake would strain to catch glimpses of lacy panties or perhaps no panties at all. Tonight Jake knew his odds were good; it was usually the case when a wild band played. Jake knew the patrons would be particularly raunchy.

"What would you do when you voyeured the women?" I ask.

"Well, I would take a snapshot in my head and save the images until I got home and then masturbate. Sometimes I'd make up stories or fantasies about them."

"To create more intensity?" I ask.

"Yes."

Although the voyeur is passively distancing himself from any intimate contact, he is, at the same time, unilaterally and aggressively appropriating a sexual privilege. The culmination of the peeping may be in orgasm achieved during the watching, or the orgasm may be delayed until the voyeur, having stored up his images, masturbates in privacy. When the pleasure is delayed and played out with stored images or euphoric recall, the template behind it has to do with an early childhood adaptation to fantasy. This will lead to a search for the origins of such an adaptation in childhood.

Voyeurism is a subtle form of empowerment without intimacy, and this is precisely how Freud analyzed it. To watch unobserved is to appropriate lives and assert oneself over one's victims. "Those we observe become ours, hostages to our eyes," wrote Sigmund Freud. The voyeur becomes a master of what he surveys, so watching becomes not only the origin of excitement, but also a remedy for pain, a reward for success, and a means for maintaining emotional balance. When in the grips of his obsession, the voyeur, even during acts of bodily sex with a real-life partner, will have to imagine a fantasy in order to reach orgasm. Real intimacy becomes impossible.

"Then you progressed into peeping in dorm windows?" I ask Jake.

"Oh, I had been peeping in windows since I was eleven; in college was the first time I got caught."

"Were you arrested?"

"No. It was just campus security, and they just gave me a slap on the hand," Jake explains.

"What was that like, when you first got caught?"

"Oh, it was awful. I was so embarrassed, but I didn't stop."

"What makes you want to get help now?" I ask.

"A lot," Jake says. "I feel like such a pervert. You just don't know what it is like to live your life trying to get a peek. It feels so desperate, so all-consuming."

"I can imagine," I say.

"I don't know how to be in a relationship. I spend all my free time either voyeuring outside or on the Net. It has ruined my life, and now I face these charges. I should have my whole life ahead of me. . . ." Jake says, his voice trailing off.

"Do you understand why you act out in this way?"

"Oh, yeah," Jake says with the confidence and enthusiasm of a schoolkid.

"I understood when I drilled that first hole in the bathroom wall. I felt the rush, the high, the power. I knew then it was wrong, but I couldn't stop then. Can't stop now. That's been the story of my life."

As a child, Jake adapted to the original wounding by creating a fantasy world in which he could escape stress and shame. Whether it is peeking under dresses in a car lot or cruising the Internet for pornography, Jake's behavior is all about his original trauma. The voyeur has adapted to avoid the emotions associated with the original wounding act.

Anonymous Sex

Anonymous sex is high-risk sex that traumatically replicates the danger posed to the child by his original perpetrator. The difference is that, in adulthood, he has become the violator in order to take power and control. It is likely that the sexual element of the danger was intense, which is how danger, sex, and intensity became fused in his sexual template.

Mark sits in the outer office of the clinic. The stark lighting irritates his eyes, and the hard chairs remind him of the demoralizing predicament that has driven him here, rather than to the comfortable office of his family practitioner.

An attractive, tall, tanned, toned, blond man in his early thirties, Mark is a stark contrast from the other patients in the waiting room. In polished Italian loafers, a designer suit with a white silk shirt, and a fashionable, abstractly patterned tie, he has the air of success.

Mark glances at his watch for the third time in five minutes. He is eager to get his appointment over because he is confident he already knows his diagnosis. Mark is all too familiar with the crushing blow that comes with the doctor's words. Like a verdict being handed down from the high court, it is something he would rather forget.

Mark can hear his uncle snoring in the twin bed across the room. He can also smell the alcohol and cigarette smoke that emanate from his breath. Uncle Joe, deemed "the biggest loser" by Mark's mother, landed on their doorstep a few days ago, jobless and broke. Mark's dad, Joe's older brother, took pity on him and agreed to help Joe get "back on his feet."

Uncle Joe's temporary lapse in snoring allows Mark to drift back to sleep. Always a sound sleeper, Mark is confused and disoriented when he is awakened again, this time by something probing his face. Still half-asleep, Mark tries to brush it away; however, this time Mark is awake enough to realize it is his uncle's penis. Mark is frantic, but his uncle restrains Mark's movement, making it impossible for him to break free. Mark feels as if he is suffocating, as if he might die, as if the violence will never end.

"Gonorrhea," Mark's doctor says. "I'm sorry to tell you, but that's what you've got."

Mark stares straight ahead as the words wash over him like a bad dream.

For Mark, the damage of his traumatic sexual wounding is a high-risk sexual addiction that is about power and control rather than sexual titillation. His high comes from the mastery over the original wounding. The problem is that, every time Mark acts out, he feels shame and is likely to sum up the feeling as self-loathing.

Mark pulls his car around the back of the building,

where there are few parking spots left. He pulls on his baseball cap, despite the fact that it is well past midnight.

The place is jumping as he opens the wooden door fashioned to look like something out of the OK Corral. Mark beelines for the back room, much seedier than the front. He knows the drill and is eager to get it started.

Mark will act out in what are called "glory holes." These are holes drilled through walls that allow penetration by an erect penis. One can be either the receiver or the giver. One man sticks his erect penis through while another man on the other side fellates him. It is dangerous, anonymous sex because neither man knows what is waiting for him on the other side, in terms of both pain and disease.

"When you heard the diagnosis, what happened for you?" I ask.

"I was humiliated."

"This has happened before?" I ask.

"Twice," Mark says, unable to make eye contact.

"Despite this humiliation, you have been unable to stop. Do you understand why?"

"Yes," he says, looking up. "It is the need to dump my anger at my drunk, perverted uncle," he says with force.

"But now you are the pervert?" I ask.

"Yes, I am the pervert," he says, letting out a long sigh.

Although Mark does not sexually assault young boys, his re-creation of the original trauma gives him the illusion of control. He is now the instigator; however, the high of becoming the perpetrator rather than the victim does nothing to heal the endemic sickness or the continual need for dysfunctional self-assertion.

Like many of the acting-out behaviors we will discuss, this type of acting out carries with it a great deal of social stigma. Often these individuals are seen, as Mark sees himself, as perverted. Society often views these people as subhuman, as rejects, or as vile and dangerous characters. These stigmas only compound the addict's shame and confusion. "Why do I choose to do this behavior? What is wrong with me that I have this kind of secret life? Why not affairs or prostitutes, like other guys? I could never tell anybody this stuff."

As we have explored, it is vital for addicts to understand their sexual templates. This part of the healing process is always fascinating. We locate and piece together the complete picture, like a puzzle needing assembly. When addicts can see the logic behind their choices of acting-out behaviors, their shameful feelings diminish. They no longer see themselves as deviant freaks, but rather as predictably damaged products of childhood wounding. Now they will be able to walk through the shame and embrace the wounded part of the self, which, despite having been driven into shameful behavior, can now be restored to hope and self-esteem.

Exploitive Sex

Exploitive sex is an overt act of power and control over someone who is vulnerable, such as the recently divorced mother of three, the salesperson depending on the boss for advancement, the person with a mental or physical disability, the college student who needs tutoring from her professor, the frail and elderly, or the child.

Usually the sexually compulsive abuser does not see himself as being exploitive; rather, he views himself as being supportive or helpful.

Chet sits in my office. He is impeccably groomed. With crisp, articulate speech, he describes the recent breakup with his partner that has brought him in for counseling.

"What do you look for in a woman?" I ask.

"That's the problem," Chet says with a sheepish expression. "I always get myself in trouble."

"How so?"

"Well, I always look for women who are somewhat wild, someone who looks like a party ready to happen," Chet says with a slight chuckle. "You know, the one who can't get enough, who wants to do it all the time, anywhere, swing from chandeliers . . . you get the idea."

"Yes, I do," I say with a slight nod.

Chet, a partner in his law firm, has found himself in several compromising situations. Seeing himself as "helpful," he likes to mentor many of his young associates—usually the ones who wear tight, short skirts.

"So the past few relationships you have been in are all with women who work for you?" I ask.

"Yes, I know it's bad," he says, pausing. "But they are always coming on to me, and what can I say? I want them to do well, to be successful, so I help them out—obviously, in more ways than one," he says with another chuckle.

"Do you think this is funny?" I ask.

"Funny? No, why?"

"Then why do you keep chuckling?" I ask.

"Because it can get so crazy."

Chet, like many who act out, is in a great deal of denial. He sees himself as a victim of the wiles of women. He feels that he's a pawn, being manipulated by their sexual come-ons.

It is a sunny, warm day as Chet plays with his toy cars in the front yard. Chet's mother, fastidious about her flower beds, is out pruning and weeding. The two, engrossed in their own worlds, are startled by the loud honk of the car driving by. Chet looks up in time to see a man hanging out of the window, ogling his mother. His mother, secretly thrilled at the attention, responds with a coy smile and a wave.

"It made me sick," Chet says with some force. "I would get so mad at those guys, I wanted to kill them."

"That is a strong reaction."

"I was really pissed," he says with continued force.

"At whom?"

Chet pauses a moment, taking a mental inventory. "I thought it was the guys, but I guess it's my mom."

Chet's feelings of shame, fear, and anger are in his throat as he watches his mom flirt. Looking over her shoulder, she moves toward the back door, shouting to Chet, "I'll be back in a few." She presses her finger to her lips, indicating that this is a secret best kept from Chet's father.

"Did she know these fellows?" I ask.

"I don't know," Chet says, shrugging his shoulders.

"Had this happened before?"

"Yeah, it had; she would just take off," Chet says with agitation in his tone.

"How would you feel?"

"Freaked out."

Chet is morbidly attracted to women over whom he can pull rank. He acts as the sexual predator his mother once appeared to be.

Children are extremely sensitive to energy. They are instinctual beings tuned into what is happening around them. It is a survival trait, and it is instinctual. For Chet, experiencing his mother's behavior was a traumatic event for several reasons. First, she was acting without appropriate sexual boundaries. Her lack of containment allowed her sexual energy to spew all over Chet like a burst fire hydrant. Chet, unable to articulate what he was feeling, knew on some level that his mother's behavior was dangerous, and a betrayal of him and his father. He felt shame and fear, and yet he had no voice.

The unconscious messages his mother sent Chet about sex were many: sex equals power and attention, sex is dangerous, sex is a weapon, sex is objectification, sex is secretive. Her behavior and nonverbal cues were the recipe that created Chet's sexual template. He learned his mother's lessons well.

Sadomasochism

Janis is an unusually active child who, in her adult years, will be diagnosed with Attention Deficit Hyperactive Disorder (ADHD). She is a handful for her parents, who have five other children. Janis's mother has no time for close supervision of her offspring.

At the age of three, Janis has taken to climbing onto the kitchen counters, over the backyard fence, up into the trees. Once her parents had to call the fire department to get her down.

Janis's mother masks her fear for Janis's safety by raging.

"She used to spank the hell out of me," Janis explains. "I know she was just afraid something would happen to me," Janis continues, "but the spankings were daily, and so were the screaming and yelling."

"What would she say?"

"Oh, she'd tell me I was a bad girl, stupid, no good, a thorn in her side, stuff like that."

When a child is spanked, especially on the bare bottom, the vibration of the impact can resound and stimulate the child's genitals. The pleasure is then merged with the pain, creating a template wherein pain and pleasure are fused.

"To try and keep me safe, she would tie me up," Janis continues.

"How would she do that?" I ask.

"Well, she used a harness and would hook it to the clothesline, so I could slide up and down the line, but I was restricted by the length of the cord tied to my waist. Or she would tie my hand or my leg to my playpen or crib."

"What was that like for you?"

"Well, first I was furious, and then I was humiliated, especially when my brothers and sisters had friends over. Then I would be tethered to the clothesline like some wild animal. If I cried or complained, my mom would come out and hit me some more."

It is dark in the dungeon as Janis puts on the finishing touches of her outfit, readying herself for her first trick of the night. She can feel the anticipation of her first session.

Her heart beats rapidly, and her mouth is dry, her breath shallow. Janis is already high as she ties the final knot into the harness.

Janis is a dominatrix. She re-creates the horrors of her childhood in her sexual torture chamber; only this time, Janis is in control.

"Sometimes I go too far," Janis says with a distant look.

"How so?" I ask.

"I just get so into it that I lose track of where I am. I just want more intensity, more pain, more humiliation. They will yell for me to stop, and I can't. I just keep going. Sometimes I scare myself. It makes me wonder what I am capable of doing."

"Are you the top (sado, the giver) or the bottom (maso, the receiver)?" I ask.

"Both."

In entering a sexual encounter, Janis does not expect nor want a loving, nurturing experience. For her, a sexual act requires danger, risk, pain, and humiliation. Janis does this because it is hardwired into her.

"Have you ever orgasmed without pain?" I ask.

"No, nor without being humiliated," she tags on as if it were an afterthought.

"I also get a better high when I am with a woman," Janis explains.

"Why do you think that is?"

"I am sure that it's because of my mother. I remember the hate I felt for her, and that's how I feel when I do a session with a woman."

Attraction to same-sex partners is often confusing for

heterosexuals; however, it is not uncommon. Addicts' choices for acting out mirror their original trauma, which often leads to behaviors that do not necessarily reflect their authentic sexual selves.

For Janis, understanding her orientation and preferences is vital for her healing process. First, it will reduce her confusion and second, it will reduce her feelings of shame. Once Janis realizes her reenactment is a mirror image of her abuse, the power will diminish, and so will the high.

"You ruined it for me," Janis says with a slight smile.

"How so?" I ask.

"You took all the fun out of it."

"You mean, once you understood why you were doing the behavior, it no longer provided a high?"

"Yes, not only does it not work, it disgusts me," she says to her own surprise.

The high that once masked Janis's shame has been replaced by the ability to feel and be present. No longer a robotic caricature of her abuse, Janis can be her true self and find healthy sexual expression.

The Cycle of Addiction

The cycle is the same for all forms of addictive behaviors. The cycle, as we have already explored, is based or grounded in a profound sense of shame and self-loathing. The shame drives the individual to take action, or move away from the pain of these feelings. The behavior used to numb the feelings of pain is based in trauma and formulated or created early in a person's life.

Patrick Carnes, in his book *Out of the Shadows,* explains this cycle. He states that, from the place of shame, an individual moves into impaired thinking, rationalization, or denial to justify his behaviors. The distorted thinking becomes automatic, like breathing. Addicts are often not aware of their justifying thoughts because the pattern has become embedded as their emotional coping mechanism. They tell themselves, "Just one more time. I am not hurting anyone. I deserve it." This rationalization gives them the green light to proceed with their behavior. Once they have given themselves permission, they will become preoccupied with the acting in or out.

This period of preoccupation creates the chemical infusion in the brain that brings great pleasure. Chemicals such as dopamine, serotonin, and adrenaline are released. For some addicts, the thinking about, planning, and anticipation of the behavior is the most pleasurable part of the cycle. When they are in this state, they are in a trance; they feel no pain. They have literally created a chemical cocktail that is as addictive as any drug.

The next part of the cycle is ritualization. All addicts have rituals, whether they are aware of them or not. Rituals reinforce and intensify the experience. Once when I was giving a lecture at The Meadows, I asked one of the clients if he had a ritual. He said, "No." I asked how he acted out, and he said he cruised for prostitutes.

"So you don't have a ritual?" I asked.

"No," he said.

"Well, where do you cruise?"

"Downtown."

"Never uptown?"

"No, always downtown."

I continued with a barrage of questions.

"Do you cruise at a specific time of day? Do you wear particular clothing? How do you carry your money? Do you drink coffee or alcohol, or smoke? Do you listen to music? What kind of woman do you look for: tall, short, large-breasted, dark skin, blonde hair?"

His answer painted a very specific ritual that came as a surprise to him as he unraveled its specifics.

"I cruise downtown, between midnight and 5 a.m. I have a cooler in my trunk where I have a bottle of vodka on ice. I have a plastic cup I got from some car wash. I place two ice cubes in the cup and sip on the vodka as I cruise. I listen to heavy metal and get my money from a specific ATM. I fold the bills in the shape of a triangle and place it in my left pocket. I wear spandex pants and dark sunglasses. It makes me feel aroused."

Intricate rituals are the norm for sex addicts. Understanding and flushing out all of the ritualized components are crucial if an addict is to move toward healthy sexual expression; each of the components is a potential trigger or cue that could send the addict back to his behaviors. The client could see a cup from the same car wash. He could hear a song he plays while cruising. Going downtown for work, he could drive by his favorite corner, or he could smell vodka.

For the acting-in, or deprivation, side of the cycle, rituals give way to distancing strategies, which can include picking a fight, making oneself unattractive, criticizing or shaming one's partner, staying busy, staying up late, medical or physical excuses such as "I have a headache; it's that time of the month," and so on. All of these strategies serve to elicit the same result: avoidance of sexual contact.

Acting in or out sexually is often not the most powerful aspect of the cycle. It is sometimes the shortest part of the cycle, whereas the majority of the time and energy go into the planning for and ritualization of the behavior. No matter where the addict seeks his most intense high, the results are always the same: feelings of shame, guilt, remorse, and despair that prompt the addict to tell himself, "I will never do this again." However, the guilt, shame, and remorse drive him back into the only coping mechanism he knows: acting out. Thus, the cycle continues until the addict's life becomes unmanageable or, as they say in twelve-step meetings, he "hits a bottom."

Hitting a bottom is a very personal experience—what you think may be a bottom for a person may not be nearly the level of pain and consequence he or she can tolerate. This is sometimes the saddest part of my work— when a client sits before me and faces what I perceive as horrendous consequences: losing a job, a partner filing for divorce and selling their home, losing visitation rights with children. Still, addicts are prisoners to the cycle.

No matter how one acts out or in, the issues and results are the same: a cycle of disruptive behaviors that becomes unmanageable and can include serious and often life-threatening consequences.

Exhibitionism

The sexual exhibitionist compulsively attracts attention to the sexual parts of his or her body, regardless of the appropriateness. We often think of the man in the trenchcoat hiding in the bushes, springing out to expose himself. But in our culture, a great deal of exhibitionism is now considered normal. There is exhibitionism at the beach, in advertising, and on television. Sexual flaunting has become so much a part of accepted culture that many sexual exhibitionists usually seek therapy only when they have gotten in trouble with family, business, or the law.

Say a man is walking down the street at night and stops and stares at a woman who inadvertently exposes herself by undressing while standing near a window in her lit bedroom with her blinds up. Chances are, if a police officer walks by, he will arrest the man as a Peeping Tom. The woman's display of nakedness so embarrasses this cop's notion of woman's Madonna-like modesty that he concludes the "always horny male" is the perpetrator.

In reality, women exhibit themselves all the time, and our culture supports this behavior, especially through sexually provocative advertising and Hollywood box-office stereotypes. So, for women, exhibitionism is often rewarded, whereas exhibitionistic men are considered perverts. This is a sad state of affairs because exhibitionism hurts everyone involved without regard to gender or sexual preference.

Often in the childhood of the sexual exhibitionist, a primary caregiver has exposed himself, causing fusion of fear and sexual arousal. Now when the victim exposes himself, he seeks to reverse the childhood trauma and banish fear and shame by becoming the perpetrator. The sexual pleasure of the perversion masks the underlying dysfunction (fear and shame), and an addiction takes hold.

It is a fine autumn day as I cut across campus. It is my first fall in the high desert, and I am surprised at how brisk the air is, despite the sunshine. I shiver as I grab the door to the main building, rushing to my office in an attempt to shake off my chill.

A group of patients has gathered outside my office, looking as if they are condemned inmates heading to the gallows. I imagine their expressions are due to feelings of anxiety about the group process that is about to begin.

Paige, the only woman in my group, pulls up the end of the procession, plopping herself down in the nearest chair. Still chilled from the 40-degree weather, I notice her multicolored sundress: sleeveless, loose-fitting, and draping to her ankles.

"Let's get started," I say, clapping my hands and attempting to help them shake off their somber expressions. "Let's get out our notebooks," I begin, "and go over. . . ." Stopping mid-sentence, I am distracted as Paige, now bending over to retrieve her notebook, has "inadvertently" exposed her bare breasts. Six men (all heterosexuals) sit with their mouths open, looking at me for some sort of a cue.

The shock felt by the victims is the high for the exhibitionist; it is where she feels power and control. This is a passive-aggressive behavior that, for women, is often couched in a naïve innocence of intention. They are exempt from responsibility because of the cultural denial that a woman would ever intentionally be so provocative. One out of four girls will be sexually assaulted by the age of eighteen. For boys, it is one out of six. We have to ask: Where does all of that sexual shame and anger get channeled? The answer is that it gets channeled into sexual compulsive behavior. Paige's behavior was intentional.

As with many of the acting-out behaviors we have discussed, the exhibitionist rarely if ever wants to be sexual. The power for her is in controlling her victims.

When Paige exposes herself, she is seeking to reverse her childhood trauma, and banish fear and shame by becoming the perpetrator. The sexual pleasure of the perversion masks her underlying sexual shame.

It is late afternoon, and Paige notices Mr. Bentley, who sits, as he always does, on a lawn chair on his front porch. Mrs. Bentley, who died three months ago after a heart attack, left emptiness in the hearts of her family members. She was the quintessential grandmother.

Paige, like all of the neighbors, had seen a fast decline in Mr. Bentley's health. To Paige, he seemed to have gone off the deep end. Two days ago, while Paige was sitting in her favorite chair across from Mr. Bentley, he had allowed his penis to be exposed in his loose-fitting shorts. At first, Paige was curious and confused, and then she was just disgusted. Paige, too embarrassed to tell anyone, let the incident go, excusing it as just an accident.

A few days later, Paige's mother made the suggestion that, while she and Paige's father were away dropping off her brother at college, Paige could stay with Mr. Bentley. She thought it would be the perfect situation because

Paige, too young to be left alone, could keep Mr. Bentley company. Paige, too afraid to tell her mother what had happened, acquiesced.

Mr. Bentley's sexual behaviors escalated immediately. Leaving the bathroom door open while he urinated, wearing the same loose shorts, and standing naked in front of Paige while she pretended to be asleep, Mr. Bentley turned Paige's stay into a horror show.

"What are you feeling, Paige?" I ask as tears stream down her face.

Her male peers, who are giving her feedback, have hit a nerve.

"I don't know; I guess sad."

"You know, Paige, I feel sad when I see you do that to yourself," says Max, one of her fellow group members. "Over the past few days, I have started to get to know you, and I think you are a valuable person. I just don't think you know it yet."

Paige bows her head in an attempt to hide her face.

"I never had anybody say these things to me," she says, tears still streaming. "I feel like such an asshole."

"Paige," I say with focus, "you are not an asshole. You are just a person who was traumatized, trying to take back your power the only way you knew how. Now you have the opportunity to learn a new way, a healthy way to heal your wounds and express your sexuality."

Intrusive Sex

Intrusive sex involves boundary violations without discovery and, although it is passive-aggressive, the energy behind the perversion is anger. A man cuts a hole in his hotel room in order to spy on the sexual goings-on of the couple next door. He could have rented a porn video if all he wanted was sexual arousal, but he wants his sexual arousal with a mandatory add-on: He has to violate the privacy boundaries of the sexual actors. His high comes from the emotions attendant on the forbidden access to what he was taught is a shameful act.

Bobby's grandmother scared him. A large woman with a booming voice, she commanded attention and seemed to suck the air out of the room. Bobby's mother was no match for her domineering mother.

"She's a nut job," Bobby's dad said.

Bobby, the youngest of five, was often left in his grand-mother's care, where he learned to stay as far from her as possible, which meant playing outside. But this, too, had its dangers. Coming home dirty would cause an uproar, and his grandmother would spank Bobby or give him a beating.

Even worse moments would occur when Bobby wet his pants. This happened frequently because Bobby was so frightened of entering the house when his grandmother was there. Bobby internalized his grandmother's shameless, red-faced rage. "You are disgusting and dirty," she would yell.

Although wetting himself was an accident born out of fear, Bobby was taught that to be himself, to be human, was to be disgusting and dirty.

After he wet himself, Bobby would be thrown into a cold bath. Scrubbing his penis with a rough cloth, his grandmother would tell him, "This is a dirty thing, a dirty thing. We have to scrub away your dirty little thing."

Bobby dared not provoke her further by crying out. He would shut his eyes, hold his breath, and wait until her fury abated.

"What are the charges?" I ask.

"Sexual harassment. There may be more; I don't know yet."

"How many charges?"

"Almost all the women in the sales department have filed a complaint."

Bobby again becomes the humiliated boy who so long ago was terrified of his grandmother. His eyes are full of fear.

The rage that Bobby had stuffed had begun to leak out by the age of ten.

"I started touching women in stores," Bobby explains. He would pretend that it was inadvertent. "I would let my hand brush up against their crotch or their butt. It was such a high."

"By ten you were doing this?"

"Yeah, I would even practice doing it in my bedroom to perfect my technique. What was so great was that, as a kid, it was so easy; they never said anything, even though I knew they felt it. The big problems started when I entered high school."

Bobby began touching girls in the crowded hallways, and making inappropriate sexual comments and obscene phone calls.

"This was before caller ID, cell phones, or any of that, but they could still trace calls," Bobby continues.

"That's the first time you got caught?"

"Yeah, when I was fourteen."

Bobby's high was in the release of his unbridled rage on unsuspecting women. Crowded hallways, public events like ball games and theater lobbies, and tight quarters such as the cabin of an airplane became prime acting-out territories.

"And then came the Internet," Bobby says. "That's when my addiction really exploded."

It's late as Bobby sits hunched over his computer; the glow of the screen is the only light in the room. Deep in concentration, he adjusts the remote cameras' focus with his keyboard controls. He has installed three cameras, one for each stall in the women's bathroom.

"Had you installed other cameras?" I ask.

"Not yet, but I had been thinking about how to install some at the women's locker room at the golf club."

Through his traumatic wounding, Bobby created a distorted sexual template that justifies his intrusive acts. In the haze of his addiction, Bobby's high comes from the emotions attendant on his forbidden access to what he was taught is dirty and shameful.

He sees women as disgusting, and he has the right to demean their sexuality the way he was demeaned. While holding himself safe from rebuke, he holds them in utter contempt, judging them from behind a wall of sexualized anger. In the one-up position of moral condemnation, he escapes the one-down position of having been condemned for the very same act. Now he is in control, and now he has the power.

Cross-dressing

When I talk about cross-dressing, I am not talking about cross-gender issues, cross-sexual issues, or what we call "she-males." I am talking about people who have an obsession, based in their trauma, to adorn themselves in the clothing of the opposite sex.

There is intense shame and secrecy associated with cross-dressing. Sometimes clients will not disclose their cross-dressing until months into their treatment because they feel it is so abnormal and shameful.

The intense, hidden anger behind cross-dressing can often be traced to the abuse a child suffered when his mother denied him the loving intimacy that is her obligation and his due. She rarely, if ever, let him get close to her. Perhaps in order to get the closeness he needs, he begins stealing her underwear. But at the same time, he exacerbates his anger with the realization that he cannot get close to her in any other way. Perhaps he masturbates while wearing her underwear, thereby fusing the intensity of sex with the shameful acts of secrecy and theft. He sexualizes his anger.

Certain addicts become transfixed on certain items of apparel. Red panties may be the only things that turn some men on. Others have to get fully dressed up. Some cross-dressers need to get high on drugs in order to indulge in their compulsion, to mask their shame and numb their pain.

Sometimes a cross-dresser, whether male or female, picks up a prostitute and has him or her cross-dress. This gives the instigating cross-dresser the experience of having sex with a man who is dressed up as a woman or with a woman who is dressed up as a man. This fantasy play conjures up the image of the original abuser, at whom the anger is directed, and becomes the erotic trigger.

❖ ❖ ❖ ❖

Joey can feel his knees throbbing as he painstakingly lays the tile in the stairway. A master tile layer, Joey considers himself an artist, as he designs, cuts, and lays each piece precisely. Left alone in the house, Joey has the opportunity to perform his sexual ritual without his usual restraints.

"What's the matter with you, my little Joey?" his mother says, picking up her crying son.

"Come here to Mama," she says, bouncing him on her hip. Madlina, only eighteen years old, adores her one-year-old son. Although she had dreamed of having a little girl, she is a doting, attentive mother.

Madlina had been collecting and making baby clothes for as long as she could remember. She kept them in a special chest she had painted by hand.

Madlina loved to make dresses; lace, ruffles, and flowers in pastel colors were her favorites. She made matching bonnets and purchased shoes and socks to pair with each outfit. Joey, with long, light, curly hair, was the perfect mannequin for Madlina's secret obsession.

Madlina put her son in the dresses. She never did this around her husband because, the one time he caught her, he became enraged. "What's the matter with you? Are you crazy?! Cut that crap out," he said, snatching up his son and ripping off the clothes.

"How long did she dress you like that?" I ask.

"Until I went to school, and, even then, she would want me to play dress-up with her."

"You remember this?"

"Oh yeah. She was a nut job, especially since I was an only child. I didn't know about the photos until I found them in her closet when I was a teenager."

"What was your reaction?"

"Shock," he says, clearly disturbed. "I couldn't believe it; then I got mad."

"Did it feel like a betrayal?"

"Big time."

When Madlina dressed her son in girl's clothes, it was an abusive act of enmeshment. Madlina used Joey to satisfy her own needs and wants. She gave Joey unwavering attention, but doing so created a sexual template for Joey that left him confused, shameful, and angry.

Joey, six-foot-two and 250 pounds, with a full beard and muscled arms, is a far cry from the delicate, feminine creature his mother attempted to cultivate.

Packing up his tools and locking them in his truck, Joey heads back into the house. Certain the owners will not return for several hours, Joey begins rummaging through the woman's lingerie drawer. Finding lacy panties, he heads over to the closet, perusing her dresses and shoes.

The intense, hidden anger behind Joey's cross-dressing is traced to the abuse he suffered when his mother denied him the loving intimacy that was her obligation and his due. It is fueled and exacerbated by his sense of betrayal and deeply embedded feelings of shame. When he masturbates while wearing stolen garments, he fuses the intensity of sex with the shameful acts of secrecy and theft. He sexualizes his anger. He feels powerful and finally in control.

Fetishism

A sexual fetish is an obsession with an object or body part that is required for sexual arousal or gratification. For the addict, the logic or connection between the body part and the obsession originates in the original trauma fused with sexual arousal.

Hon sits in front of the fan, watching the blades whiz. He is transfixed as he attempts to make out each blade as it turns.

"Come over here and help me," Hon's mother snaps.

She has pulled out the card table for her weekly mahjong game.

"Thank you, my good son," she says with a smile. "Now help me set up the chairs."

Four-year-old Hon resents these weekly gatherings. His mother, a single parent who works during the week, has little time or energy to spend with Hon. On Saturdays she spends her afternoons playing mahjong with her family and friends. For hours on end, they sit, chatting and playing, leaving Hon isolated and uncared for.

Like many of the behaviors we have explored, in our culture, fetishism carries tremendous shame and invites scornful abuse that drives the addict into a secret and sordid life.

The fixation can be as varied as the individuals. I once heard a colleague say that a sex addict can become addicted to anything in the Sears and Roebuck catalog. This is probably true, and it is my job to help make sense of why this is so. Once addicts are able to understand their connection with the objects that compulsively enslave them, their shame will automatically reduce, and the power the objects hold will diminish.

Hon has crawled under the table. The light, filtering through the red, floor-length tablecloth, affords him a secret world. Underneath the table, he feels safe, as if in a cocooned womb. The smells are fragrant, the bare legs are soft and supple, and the brightly painted toenails, all fire-engine red, fixate Hon's attention.

Even more curious are the short skirts, revealing a triangular shadow between tightly held thighs. Hon strains to see what secrets lie beneath.

"When did your foot fetish begin?" I ask Hon.

"As long as I can remember," he responds, adjusting his crooked glasses on the brow of his nose.

"You mentioned last week you thought it was linked to your mother?"

"Definitely."

"How did you feel when your mother had her Saturday parties?" I ask.

"I felt totally rejected; it was always about her, what she wanted."

"Did you feel controlled by her?"

"Controlled and rejected."

"A painful combination," I say.

Under the table, Hon feels excitement and danger. He knows his curious obsession is wrong, but the power he feels when acting out is addictive. The only time Hon is able to act out is on Saturdays, when the women take their seats at the card table. Hon's fantasies about his secret world dance through his head; the smells, the red dancing toes, the supple legs, and the crotches become obsessions.

"You would solicit the women directly?"

"Yes, I did. When all the elements came together, I had this overwhelming urge. I know it was crazy; I was like a madman, but I had to do it."

"Where would you do this?" I ask.

"I did it everywhere—stores, restaurants. My favorite places are casinos. It gives me the same feeling as when I was a kid."

The excitement Hon feels when he cruises provides the intensity he felt as the "naughty" boy under his mother's table. But this time, he has the power to unleash the anger he could not aim at his mother. Hon is no longer the victim, the rejected little boy. He is the man driven to take back, to retrieve what was his due.

Bestiality

Bestiality is the addictive attraction to or interaction with an animal for sexual arousal. The basis for this behavior is the same as for the other acting-out behaviors we have explored; it is derived from trauma fused with sexual shame.

It is early morning as the sun rises over the fields. The frost on the ground dances like tiny crystals. Pete has been up for nearly an hour and is well into cleaning stalls and distributing hay. He can see his breath as he moves mechanically through his chores.

Pete has just turned thirteen and, despite his love of the land and the work, he aches for emotional connection. His mother is a cold woman who has raised Pete and his sisters in the tradition of "spare the rod and spoil the child." His father does not suffer fools lightly either. He is rigid, self-righteous, and emotionally distant.

The only boy in a family of six, Pete has been treated like a hired hand, his emotional needs ignored. Long ago, he developed an emotional connection to the animals. He learned to channel his emotional ache into their care and attention. The animals and their cycles of life became a natural undercurrent shaping Pete's own development. The copulation in the fall and resulting births in the spring were a natural curiosity in Pete's sexual development.

"When did you first act out with an animal?" I ask Pete.

Obviously uncomfortable, Pete responds, "I guess I was around thirteen or fourteen years old."

"It sounds like, as a kid, you were starved for emotional attention and comfort."

"I wouldn't say 'starved,'" Pete says in a defensive tone, as if admitting an emotional need would put his character in question. "But I was lonely."

Pete, who was recently arrested for having sex with the cows on his neighbor's dairy farm, has landed in my office. With his neighbor threatening to sue and the county ready to prosecute, Pete is facing the harsh consequences of his addiction.

"My life is a mess," Pete says in a defeated tone.

"That is one way of looking at it, but now you have the opportunity to get help."

"There is no help; I'm just a perverted sexual deviant," he says, rubbing his face with his hands as if trying to rub his shame away.

"No, you are a man who, as a young boy, found a way to ease his loneliness."

"Good God, stop with the psychobabble. I could end up in jail."

Pete's defensive posture was born from his lack of trust in others. As a child, he was taught self-sufficiency, to endure and perform. He learned to abandon his authentic self by denying his emotional truth. He learned to toe the line, pull his weight, and bury his emotions.

"Do you think you resented the lack of emotional connection you had with your parents?" I ask.

"Probably," he says, a little less defensively.

"And that you acted that anger out in your secret sexual world?"

"Probably," he says in a softer tone.

Pete's lack of emotional connection left him desperate for attention, love, and connection. The only overt affection he knew was with the animals. They provided him with loyalty and unconditional love. Through them he found connection.

The imprint of Pete's parents' emotional neglect was profound. As his anger at his parents simmered and his curiosity about sexual development progressed, his perversion began to fester and grow.

When Pete received the attention and loyalty of the animals, he knew they were vulnerable. But, at the same time, he felt driven to violate them. He did this in an attempt to control his parents' emotional abuse and neglect, which he was unable to control. The very thing Pete so desperately craved, he debased.

"Then that is what we need to work on: the anger and shame you felt as that lonely boy," I say.

This is where Pete will find his healing—through the emotional connection he lost so long ago, a connection that can ultimately restore Pete to a sense of worth and value.

Chapter 8

CULTURAL CONDITIONING: MADONNAS, WHORES, PRINCES, PLAYBOYS, AND PERVERTS

We are a culture that uses sex like a drunk uses alcohol. We stimulate ourselves with sexual fantasies, innuendo, bragging, and mockery, all in order to medicate the unacknowledged shame of our failures at sexual intimacy.

Our sexual sideshows can get bizarre. Janet Jackson exposes her breast at the halftime show of the Super Bowl, or Britney Spears and Madonna tongue each other on national television. We respond to these exploits with a shiver of naughtiness and then beg for more.

We have the opportunity to experience our sexuality as the sacred energy force it is. This source of life and energy can be channeled into our relationships, giving them power, creativity, and healthy self-care. I will discuss this sacred life energy in greater detail in Chapter 11, but first I want to explore the dysfunctional cultural beliefs about sexuality that have come to dominate our psyches.

These messages are not only generated from the mass marketing machine. In churches, sex is "bad and sinful." In schools, fourth-grade girls are pressured to dress in sexually provocative attire. On sports teams, the messages are: "Tough it out," "Only sissies cry," and "Don't act like a fag."

Stereotypes are born from these everyday slogans, cheap opinions, and bigotry. What about the boy who is homosexual? Where does he fit in? Or the girl who is taught to deny her feelings when she falls down and skins her knee? Or the youngster who is ridiculed because he would rather study than chase "ass?" The beauty of individual expression is devalued, and irresistible pressure is exerted to join the "normals" in the pursuit of sexually dysfunctional stereotypes. One of these stereotypes is called "the Madonna/whore split."

Madonnas and Whores

The Madonnas are the mothers to our children, the pillars of our families, and the goddesses of our communities. They are pure. The Madonnas shun the dark side of human sexuality and banish the whores to hell. We put the Madonnas on a pedestal, and we can't think of them as being sexual or sexy because they must be pure. They must be virginal like the Madonna herself.

And then we have the whores—the girls "we can play with." These girls are promiscuous and seductive, and culturally we think of them as wrong and bad. By calling them these names, we scapegoat them and transfer our sexual shame to them. We think they are kinky curiosities, seducers, and nymphos. The labels dehumanize them. Our contact with them is for physical gratification or pornographic imagining, only there is no intimacy. We think they are beneath us although we have paid the price of grandiosity by denying their humanity and our own lust. In this acting-in behavior, we self-righteously attack the whore, who is our shadow self.

The whores are seen as sexual objects, cheap, tawdry, trashy seductresses who lure our men into unspeakable realms. The whores are usually associated with the acting-out part of the cycle. Culturally, they are considered loose, easy, and disposable. They are not respected but are secretly desired as they provide the elixir for the virile male's unfulfilled fantasies and lust.

Whores are sexual performers who usually dissociate before, during, and after sex. Often the chase, rather than genital contact or orgasm, is the most exciting part of the process. They seek pleasure in taunting, teasing, and punishing their "prey." They see men as their victims, as weak, stupid, and disposable. They use their sexuality as a weapon, not for pleasure but for punishment. They feel in charge and powerful.

Men are afraid of the whore because of the emotional and/or physical danger, but, as addicts, they seek her because she is a playground for their shadow material. The fear creates emotional and/or physical danger. They become addicted to the intensity because it re-creates the same emotions that were provoked by their original trauma.

We cannot have the whore in our everyday lives. Instead, we want Madonna, and so our women have learned to be Madonnas, all at a terrible cost. For decades we have had cultural icons who act out for us, such as Marilyn Monroe or Christina Aguilera, who blast their sexuality in our faces like a highway billboard. In our culture, they become sexual caricatures. We tuck them away until they are needed for a sexual high. We do not let the sexuality that they imply— and that we affirm by granting them celebrity—take place in our own bedrooms. That would be shameful.

We have been conditioned to deny the human totality of our sexuality, which creates no less a delusion than denying our reason, our compassion, our hunger, or our need for friendship and intimacy. So sex is split between the pure and the sinful.

In our culture, the burden of sexual shame is most brutal to women, whose Madonna-hood has been forced upon them by male dominance. Why is it that many women cannot have fun around their sexuality? Why is it that they cannot freely orgasm? Why is it that they cannot feel good about their bodies? It is because of shame. It is because "good girls don't do that."

The cultural conditioning that honors the denial of authentic sexuality has sexually disempowered the Madonnas. Often the idea of self-pleasuring and orgasm is an unobtainable and unimaginable reality: the forbidden fruit. This repression can generate passive-aggressive behaviors, which can include withholding sex, controlling sex, or keeping secrets, such as faking orgasms or dissociation. Passive-aggressive thoughts might include, "I will pleasure my partner, but he had better provide and take care of me and/or give me what I want. If not, there will be hell to pay."

Sex with a partner can become something that is obligatory and/or tedious. Madonnas often feel trapped. This generates resentments, which justify revenge.

Many heterosexual men are afraid of the Madonnas because they were abused or emasculated by their mothers. They live in silent and/or unconscious terror that their partners will eventually retaliate, humiliate, or abandon them. To protect themselves from this inevitability, they flip-flop between a "wall of pleasant" caretaking and a "wall of anger." In the caretaking mode, they expect to be appreciated and emotionally safe. When a relational conflict arises, it triggers them back into the terror of their original wounding, and they mask their fear with a wall of anger. They have an affair, they see prostitutes, or they look at porn and masturbate while their partner is asleep—all in secret, all in anger, all fueled by the fear and inadequacy imparted by childhood wounds.

We are not adequately looking at this cultural shame. We are not adequately addressing what goes on in women's bodies, minds, and souls, or what they want sexually. Many women don't know themselves. They have been shamed out of their sexual gift, and this shaming away of sexual human reality is epidemic.

Certainly the women I treat are not getting a sexual education rooted in the fullness of their admirable humanity. Knowing the truth about their humanity—its virtues and imperfections—allows acceptance and self confidence of sexual vitality to flourish.

I do not think we are aware of how we have scapegoated women, how we have shamed them from becoming the full sexual human beings they were created to be.

Some women who come in to talk to me present the Madonna–whore syndrome. I ask them if they have ever had an orgasm; they tell me never. They tell me they don't enjoy sex. I ask if they have ever masturbated, and they tell me no. They don't know how to masturbate, and the idea sounds dirty and shameful. They tell me they are afraid to masturbate, afraid to orgasm.

I also treat female clients who are at the other extreme: women who have acted out and are the "bad" girls. They feel shamed and dirty. Often they are depressed because of this shame, because of their inability to embrace the human reality of their sexuality and to know how they have been abused. In the myth, the objects of male sexual buccaneers are women who enjoy the attention and who are empowered by their ability to seduce. Men arouse themselves in private with these delusions of sexual potency. Unconscious of these compelling myths about male and female sexuality, both males and females accept their roles within the myths. They honor a split between the whores and the Madonnas, who represent the chaste and honorable soul of womanhood. The Madonnas point their fingers in shame at the lack of character and self-respect of the whores.

In my own Irish Catholic heritage, my mother's sexuality was intensely shame-based. When I was growing up in the '70s, all of the girls were getting bikinis, wearing halter-tops, and baring their midriffs. I wanted be part of that scene and my peer culture. My mother told me I absolutely could not. I had to beg to get a two-piece swimming suit, because, according to my mother, bad girls wear those kinds of things. Good girls don't.

When I first entered treatment, I saw the men around me as perpetrators—the worshippers and creators of the whores. But if this was so, why was I relating to these men with whom I sat in treatment? Why was I relating so clearly to their feelings of loneliness, pain, and shame? Why was I relating to their sexualized anger?

As my recovery and knowledge progressed, I began to see the same individual and cultural patterns of denial I had experienced in my own process. When I stepped into the professional realm and began training therapists, I was surprised at how many professionals also accepted the psychological myth of the Madonna–whore split. It became alarmingly clear that, if clinicians were treating females as either the Madonna or the whore, then these women were not receiving the treatment, support, and healing they needed.

The Prince, the Playboy, and the Pervert
The Prince

Men, too, live in a culture that mythologizes and falsifies their sexuality. The "Prince" is a fantasy created in the minds of women, who are conditioned to be emotionally needy and dependent on the virile male.

Gail, who is in treatment for her sexual acting-out behavior, is a woman strong in character. She is self-employed, earning over half a million dollars a year. She is intelligent, articulate, energetic, attractive, and successful. On the outside she has it all: a beautiful home, nice cars, and a successful business career. Internally, however, her world is very different.

Inside, Gail feels empty, alone, and anxious. She believes she is not deserving of love.

"What is it that you want in a relationship?" I ask.

"I want him to take care of me," she says.

"What would that look like?"

"I could become a lady of leisure; you know, go to the gym, lunch with girlfriends, shop, decorate the house," she says, somewhat surprised that I do not seem to be sharing the bliss of her vision.

"That is how you want to be in relationship with your partner?"

"Yes, taken care of."

What Gail wants is a parent, not a partner. She wants her partner to step in and rescue her from the responsibilities of being an adult. She wants a knight in shining armor, a savior. Not only does she want this, she also believes it is her due.

For years she has bought into the cultural reinforcement that when she grows up, men will keep her safe, à la Barbie and Ken dolls. The fantasy develops into a defined image, which includes a prince who is charming, daring, bold, strong, and sensitive. He will listen, understand, and give her what she wants emotionally. He is among the "nice" men who make sacrifices for their women. They are expected to be sexually experienced, and, if he perceives a fault in his woman, he would never disclose it to her because he is too sensitive and gallant.

When the fantasy bursts, there is rage, outcry, disbelief, betrayal, retaliation, and revenge. Women support each other in the sorority of "man hating." They feel justified in doing so, thinking, "What do you expect? Men only want one thing." Having assumed the victim stance, the women restart the cycle by seeking out a new prince to ease their pain.

The individual leaving denial and grieving the myth is paramount in the healing process, which is usually excruciatingly painful. Often the woman will drop into a soul death, where she feels as if the very essence of her being has been made worthless. Often there are suicidal thoughts or gestures. This grief process is also tinted with a sense of betrayal: the cultural betrayal of the lost fantasy. In order for a woman to heal, she must learn how to construct an internal self that is sexually affirming and part of a healthy relationship. (Much of this will be discussed in Chapter 11.)

The Playboy

In the myth of the "playboy," men are encouraged and expected to be sexually virile, assertive, assured, and successful. From a very early age, a man is taught that his penis and his sexuality are entities separate from other aspects of his humanness. A man's sexuality and genitals are dissociated or disconnected from his otherwise complex humanity. The genitals seem to have a life of their own, exempt from responsibility and relationship. Playboys have an emotionally abstract argot for sex and genitalia: "Did you get 'it'—get laid, get pussy, get some tail, get a piece?"—a playboy might ask. They refer to their penises as "Woody," "Sparky," "Johnson," and "Mr. Midnight." Women are objects to be conquered, status symbols to be acquired, "a good time," a little relaxation to take the edge off a tough day on the job. This kind of "manly cleverness" is not only encouraged, it is often revered.

The Pervert

Sexually offending and fetish behaviors are considered perverted, deviant, a nuisance, and subhuman. Sexual offenders become cultural scapegoats for the sexual shame we feel when we deny the full reality of human sexuality. Anyone who has been the victim of sexual abuse has the capacity to switch from victim to perpetrator. But it is more comfortable to be in denial about the childhood origins of sexual deviation. After all, no one likes to accuse parents of "not loving" their children, and no one wants to give a pervert the excuse that he was a victim rather than willingly evil.

Our shame is triggered when we hear the story of the high-school teacher who has sex with his fourteen-year-old student. Our initial feeling may be disgust or anger, but, at a deeper level, what we feel is the shame of our sexual shadow side, our inner perpetrator. We then project this shame onto the offender. Our righteous condemnation is considered normal and is culturally supported. We look away in disbelief, disgust, and intolerance. "How can anyone have been so vile?" we ask, and then walk away so as not to get the answer.

The solution will be found in unmasking our cultural myths. Once we are able to deconstruct our cultural and personal denial, we will promote and pursue the restoration of authentic sexual expression, which finds its reward in healthy intimacy with self and others.

Chapter 9

HIGH-PROFILE CASES IN CONGRESS AND THE CHURCH

ex addicts' need for more intense highs drives them into realms they swore to themselves would always be off-limits. Sometimes their offenses become socially notorious, making headlines and filling the nightly television news. Two recent examples of such notoriety are the sexual predation of young males by priests of the Roman Catholic Church, and the case of Congressman Mark Foley, who was outed as a sex offender targeting young males.

As I have argued throughout this book, sexual addiction originates in the psychological damage suffered by children at the hands of primary caregivers. It leads to compulsive sexual offenses that become more frequent. As we have already explored, sexual perpetration occurs more often than is commonly thought. At the Women of

Substance website, the nonprofit organization's statistics present a painful reality:

- Among girls, 38 percent are sexually abused before the age of eighteen.
- Among boys, 16 percent are sexually abused before the age of eighteen.
- In 1994, 345,000 sexual abuse incidents were reported to Child Protective Services in the United States.
- Of all sexual abuse cases, 90 to 95 percent go unreported to the police.
- In most cases, the child knows the sex offender. With female victims, 29 percent of the offenders were relatives, and 60 percent were acquaintances.
- With male victims, 16 percent of the offenders were relatives, and 44 percent were acquaintances.

We Want the Truth!!! Waterboard GOP Mark Foley Now!

—*Washington Post*

Priest Says He, Foley Had Encounters

—*USA Today*

The headlines glared out from newsstands, and questions were asked. What about the case of Mark Foley, a man who led a double life, whose secret world came crashing in on him in a publicly humiliating scandal?

Mark Foley, born in Newton, Massachusetts, on September 8, 1954, was one of six children. He was baptized in the Catholic Church, and his godfather, Jimmy Piersall, a retired player for the Boston Red Sox, was a close friend of the family. His father relocated the family to Lake Worth, Florida, when Mark was three. Mark's youth was spent in the quiet community, where he eventually helped his mother open a family restaurant called The Lettuce Patch. His political aspirations began when he was appointed to the Lake Worth City Council at the age of twenty-three.

Foley, a six-term congressman for the state of Florida, easily won his seat in two elections by receiving more than 60 percent of the vote. Foley was a member of the powerful House Ways and Means Committee and, throughout his political career, was an advocate and activist for the protection of youth from sexual predators.

Foley was one of the foremost opponents of child pornography serving on the House Caucus of Missing and Exploited Children. In 2002, he introduced a bill to outlaw websites that showed sexually suggestive images of preteens. In 2003, he sent a letter to the governor and attorney general of Florida, requesting that they review the legality of a program for nudist teenagers in Land O' Lakes, Florida. Foley's legislation, which changed federal sex offender laws, was supported by a number of victims' rights groups, including The National Center for Missing and Exploited Children, and John Walsh, host of *America's Most Wanted* and father of Adam Walsh, who was abducted at the age of six and has never been found.

President George W. Bush signed Foley's bill as part of the Adam Walsh Child Protection and Safety Act of 2006. Foley was also involved in getting a law passed that allows volunteer youth-serving organizations to have access to

FBI fingerprint background checks for the safety of the children involved.

So what happened? How did the career of Mark Foley—whose external world appeared devoted to the protection and safety of children—end in such scandal?

In Foley's case, I can only guess at what drove him to such sexual offending.

Mark, an altar boy at Sacred Heart Catholic Church in his hometown of Lake Worth, was abused by a parish priest. Father Anthony Mercieca, a trusted authority figure, admitted sexually abusing Mark from age thirteen to age fifteen.

In several interviews reported by the press, Mercieca described the offenses in terms that indicate his denial and justification of his behaviors. "We were friends," he said, "and trusted each other as brothers and loved each other as brothers. It was not what you call intercourse...there was no rape or anything...maybe light touches here and there." In another interview, Mercieca reported, "He seemed to like it, you know? So it was sort of more like a spontaneous thing." In yet another interview, he talked about a number of sexual encounters that "Foley might perceive as sexually inappropriate," such as "massaging Foley while the boy was naked, skinny-dipping together at a secluded lake in Lake Worth, and being naked in the same room on overnight trips."

As of October 25, 2006, Mercieca faced further accusations of sexual abuse by another altar boy, who was twelve at the time of his alleged abuse.

As we have already explored, denial, distorted thinking, and justification are a large part of the addictive cycle. In his statements, Mercieca indicates he is unable to comprehend his offenses and the damage they caused his victim. He speaks of intimacy, friendship, and trust, thus demonstrating his delusion.

A common pattern for sexual offenders is the grooming of their victims, meaning they lure them into sexual traps. They are highly skilled at building trust with the children; techniques include engaging in common interests, offering advice, and seeming to care and emotionally support the children. In an offender's mind, these acts are rarely if ever spontaneous; they are usually planned and executed in a premeditated, systematic pattern. The offender's grooming techniques can be very confusing to the child, and they most assuredly result in feelings of extreme betrayal.

The child who is seduced into the offender's trap sees the authority figure as caring, loving, and concerned. He likes the attention and believes that the groomer's intentions are sincere. Before he knows it, he is being sexually abused. Sexuality becomes traumatically associated with betrayal and terror. A lifelong scar is made.

In the offender's web, the child bonds with the illusion of a trusted confidant. At the onset of the abuse, the victim experiences profound confusion: "This is my friend. He cares about me, and friends who care shouldn't hurt me." Victims internalize the problem as being about them rather than the offender: "I must deserve this. This must be a good thing; there is something wrong with me for not liking it." The confusion is further compounded by the physical pleasure (the body responds no matter the source of stimulation and is unable to discern "good" from "bad" touch). But emotionally, the child feels afraid and confused. His or her reality becomes distorted as the youngster learns to doubt him or herself. This distrust and distortion of reality are the birth of the shame core, the bed in which all addictions are born.

The next question the media raised was: Did Foley's abuse cause his offenses? If we apply the theory that all abused children have the potential to become the abuser, then the answer, in the case of Foley, is probably yes.

All sexual abuse survivors are set up to offend, first themselves and then their victims. Do all sexually abused children become sexual predators? They do not. But it is safe to say that all people who are sexually abused will have painful emotions around their sexuality, and they will be called on to confront their abuse during their recovery.

The press also raised the question: Did Foley's sexual abuse make him gay? Again, the question can be answered only in hypothetical terms. Our theory indicates that individuals who act out with same-sex partners, and who were abused by someone of the same sex, are often repeating the pattern of abuse in an attempt to work through or resolve the original wound. The behavior does not always indicate sexual orientation. This confusion is a common issue in treatment for individuals who are in primary relationship with someone of the opposite sex but who act out with someone of the same sex. What is crucial in the treatment is the resolution of the client's truth.

In the reporting or discussion of offending sexual behaviors, the terminology describing an offense can easily be misused or misunderstood. These terms include "pedophile," "ephebofile," and "hebefile." The *Diagnostic and Statistical Manual of Diagnostic Disorders (DSM)* lists these diagnostic criteria for pedophilia:

A. Over a time of at least six months, recurrent, intense sexually arousing fantasies, sexual urges, or behaviors involving sexual activity with a prepubescent child or children (generally age thirteen and younger).
B. The fantasies, sexual urges, or behaviors cause clinically significant distress or impairment in social, occupational, or other important areas of functioning.
C. The person is at least sixteen years old and at least five years older than the child.

(Note: Do not include an individual in late adolescence involved in an ongoing sexual relationship with a twelve- or thirteen-year-old.)

The terms "ephebofile" and "hebephile" are often used interchangeably within the justice system. They are not delineated in the *DSM* but are defined as individuals who are primarily attracted to pubescent and/or postpubescent adolescents.

An individual may offend in an undifferentiated manner, meaning he or she will be attracted to kids of all ages and both genders. However, this is usually not the case. Most offenders who were sexually abused will abuse children who are within one to two years of the age of their own abuse. Foley was abused between the ages of thirteen and fifteen. His only identified victim was sixteen at the onset of the abuse.

The fact that Congressman Foley's sexual trauma was inflicted on him by a parish priest raises inevitable questions and contemplation of the widespread sexual abuse within the Roman Catholic Church.

Archdiocese Hid Abuse, Grand Jury Says

—Boston Globe

More glaring headlines streaked across the nation, sending a resounding wave of shock and outrage.

Abuse Cost Churches Nearly $467M in '05

—Boston Globe

17 Priests Reported Discipline in Long Island Sex Abuse Cases??

—New York Times

Every day the reports appeared, they described the unraveling of a great institution, once a place of sacred healing and truth.

In 2004, 1,000 Alleged Abuse by Priests

—Washington Post

Priest Guilty in Sex Abuse of 11-Year-Old Altar Boy

—New York Times

Priest Suspended After Sex Abuse Accusations

—New York Times

The fallout, which began in earnest in 2002, was staggering. "The figures released yesterday," reported the

Washington Post on February 19, 2005, "bring the total number of alleged victims since 1950 to 11,750, and the church's expenses to more than $840 million. Three diocese have declared bankruptcy."

As the reports continued to appear, the numbers became even more staggering.

"The church's cumulative expenditures on child sex abuse claims in the United States are now approaching $1.5 billion," reported the *Spokesman Review.*

How could an institution that we trusted, that we looked to for guidance, that held the salvation of our souls, be responsible for such horrors? Like a dam bursting, cover-ups, lies, and deceit resulted in a catastrophic gush that overflowed the banks. It eroded the deception, exposing that which had been buried, like the corpses deep in the bowels of the church's crypts. Thousands of victims, once silenced, hiding in the shame of secrecy, could now speak. Their voices lifted, and a deafening cry was heard as the multitude of violations was proclaimed.

How could this be—the church churning out sex offenders, each accusation more horrid than the last? Questions were asked, answers sought. Is it the environment? Are the priests gay? Words such as "pedophile" and "ephebofile" appeared in TV anchor scripts. But what did this all mean? How do we understand such atrocity?

Is there a specifically sexual component in church life that has caused such sexual acting out?

To understand priestly sexual misconduct, we must recognize that priests are no different than other individuals in terms of sexual development. Like all children, they develop their sexual templates through their sexual experiences—conscious and unconscious, overt and covert.

The things that were done to a priest were done by the usual suspects—his childhood caregivers—and in ways I have described throughout this book. The question is not only "How can a priest have done such a thing?" It is also "How can someone have done such a thing to the priest?" The fact that the offender is a priest does not create a separate class for his kind of sexual acting out or offending.

What kind of parenting are priests likely to have had? And if that parenting was abusive, what in church life encouraged its unhealthy growth? Like all abuse survivors, young priests live and react from their shame core. If they are survivors of abuse, they do not have the tools to be self-empowering and accountable. Not having a positive sense of self, they will characteristically react as having been victimized—by everything bad that happens in life—in the church and out. The adult wounded child goes into a victim stance as a way of coping with his lack of personal skills and power.

Some stay in the "poor me" victim stance, whereas others flip into aggressive offenses. From the victim's stance they do not ask what their role was in the abuse, or what they need to do in order to take care of themselves, they attack from the victim's stance. From either the victim's or agressive stance, all abuse takes place, not only priestly abuse. These attacks take the victim from one-down to one-up. Addiction, which is always a one-up posture, is often concomitant with the victim stance.

Richard Sipe, a psychotherapist and former

Benedictine monk and priest, has researched the institution and practice of priestly celibacy for more than thirty years. He contends that the culture within the church does affect the emotional maturity and sexual expression of the individual. In his book *Sex, Priests and Power*, he writes:

Priests may be ordinary men, as stated in the 1972 Kennedy-Heckler study of priesthood, but they do not exist in an ordinary social-moral culture. Theirs is a culture apart. It is an exclusively male world bounded by mandatory celibacy, where power, control, employment and even financial reward are dependent on the exclusion of women and the appearance of a sex-free existence. No one can say that this culture has nothing to do with the problem of child sexual abuse. Experience demonstrates clearly that cultural factors inherent in the celibate/sexual system are crucial and pivotal in some instances of sexual abuse, not only of minors but also women and men.

Sipe also states that 70 percent of priests who sexually abuse others were themselves abused as children, some by priests. As we have already explored, a traumatized person will react or adapt to his abuse, often re-creating it from the power position. This re-creation is an attempt to have power, control, or mastery over the original trauma. If a sexually abused individual enters the priesthood—a system that Sipe reports is an abnormal social-moral culture—his sexual health will continue to be arrested, meaning he will be more likely to remain in the adapted self. Or his behavior may worsen or progress if untreated in this environment.

Sipe's research also reports that 2 percent of the priest population can be classified as true pedophiles, with a three-to-one preference for boys. Four percent of the priest population sexually offends adolescents. Gender preference is distributed more evenly in this group.

With the onslaught of reports of sexual abuse in the Catholic Church, it is my hope that the church will examine the role its culture plays in a priest's sexual maturity. Hopefully, the church will question how it might grow and enhance the well-being and health of not only the individual, but the institution as a whole.

It is important to note that sexual abuse is not limited to Catholic priests or politicians. I have used these cases as examples because of the recent play they have received in the popular media. These incidents serve as a springboard for exploring the larger issues of sexual offending and treatment. Sexual abuse always has and probably always will cross all political, economic, gender, sexual orientation, social, intellectual, religious, racial, and ethnic lines.

Terminology and Treatment

In terms of treatment, the word "offending" can be defined in two ways: linguistically and legally. As we have already explored, it means to violate boundaries— physically, emotionally, sexually, or spiritually. For the addict, boundary violation is often done to increase the high or to test limits; he is provocative by making sexually suggestive overtures, or she attempts to shock by telling lewd or embarrassing jokes.

In legal terms, a sexual offense is the violation of a law. Offending behavior that breaks a law always falls into both categories: a boundary violation and a legal offense.

The laws and their consequences or legal judgments vary from state to state. Treatment also varies, given the type of offense and the history of an individual's behavior. When assessing patients who have acted out in legal terms, I want to explore their histories of acting out. Was there a progression to the behavior, and did it follow the cycle of addiction? I also compare their behaviors against a continuum. These behaviors exist on three levels, which are defined by both social and legal parameters.

Level One

These behaviors are legal and generally seen as culturally acceptable; however, they can be devastating when used compulsively.

- Masturbation
- Serial relationships
- Adult pornography
- Cybersex (chat rooms, stories)
- Affairs
- Fantasy
- Cross-dressing

Level Two

These behaviors are significantly intrusive and illegal but are often viewed as "nuisance" offenses.

- Voyeurism
- Exhibitionism
- Indecent liberties
- Prostitution
- Strip clubs
- Massage parlors
- Bestiality

Level Three

These behaviors violate the most significant boundaries. If caught, the perpetrators can face severe legal consequences.

- Rape
- Incest
- Molestation
- Cybersex (involving underage children or adolescents)

In the assessment process, I look for patterns and treatment modalities that can best serve the patient. It is important to note that there have been two approaches to treating sexual offenders. The first is "the offender's model," largely used in criminal settings such as with incarcerated or paroled clients. This model has historically been a cognitive/behavioral model, meaning it addresses the thoughts that generate the individual's behavior. The cognitive/behavioral model can be an effective modality. Many treatment centers and practitioners are expanding their programs, as explained by Barbara Schwartz in the book *The Sex Offender: Corrections, Treatment and Legal Practice,* "Society cannot afford to lock up all offenders forever. Instead, it should determine how offenders can be rehabilitated using a 'whole system' or 'integrative' approach to treatment."

An integrated model is more congruent with the "addictions model" used at The Meadows because it focuses on the patient's behavior as it relates to his underlying trauma. The goal is the integration of the whole person: body, mind, and spirit.

No matter what model or combination of models is implemented, each case needs individual assessments to determine appropriate treatment planning to best serve the patient's long-term treatment goals.

That assessment needs to include the patient's psychosocial history, his capacity for victim empathy, and his willingness to change, including compliance with treatment and the integration of all levels of recovery.

Other factors that can come into play include:

- **The patient's mental health status.** Is he mentally able to participate in treatment? Blocks may include psychotic breaks, levels of dissociation, and antisocial traits.
- **Socioeconomic limits.** Does he have a means of transportation to get to treatment?
- **Organic brain damage,** the causes of which may include excessive drug use or head injury.

- **Cognitive functioning.** Does he have the mental capacity to follow complex thought patterns and insight orientation? Is he able to connect his process to an emotional internal world?

For some sexual offenders, treatment may consist of a functional process, whereas a deeper integrated experience will be appropriate for others. Fortunately, the fields of sexual offending treatment and sexual addiction treatment continue to grow, adding to their programs progressive materials for advancing the health of each patient.

One effective tool, "the typologies of offenders," was introduced in 1979 by Dr. Nicholas Groth. He divided sex offenders into two categories. The first is the regressed, or situational, offender. These individuals are more impulsive; their triggers for acting out are usually external and related to stress, such as getting a bad review at work or having a fight with their partner. Their offending behaviors usually fall in Level Two.

The second typology is the fixated offender. These offenders are less impulsive, planning their offenses over time. They are usually not under the influence of mood-altering chemicals, and their behaviors usually fall in Level Three.

The treatment outcome for the regressed, or situational, offenders who are motivated in treatment is usually positive. Often the regressed offender started acting out with legal behaviors but progressed into illegal behaviors. These patients usually have the capacity for victim empathy, can feel remorse, and, once the consequences are steep enough, are willing to work in a treatment program.

For the fixated offender, there has usually been no progression in the offending behaviors. Their offensive behaviors have remained constant over time, and often there is little to no victim empathy. The treatment modality for these clients is slightly different; the focus often is on building remorse, victim empathy, behavioral tasks, and accountability for behavior.

It is important that these wounded and suffering individuals receive the treatment they need, that our culture recognizes the prevalence of sexual perpetrations, and that we challenge ourselves to face the issue from an educated, rather than a purely reactive, stance. As a culture, we must collectively address these devastating issues. This does not by any means condone offending behaviors, but rather challenges our paradigm, calling for continued explorations and answers that serve to promote positive and life-affirming actions.

Chapter 10

HEALTHY SEXUALITY

ealthy sexuality is what we hope sexual recovery brings. We are often overwhelmed by the idea of "healthy" sex. The answers to questions such as, "What is healthy sexual expression, and how does a person determine when his or her sexual behavior is compulsive?" can feel like cosmic mysteries. The recovering sex addict is not only intimidated by but afraid of the challenges of healthy intimacy.

The answers, however, are much simpler than most of us realize. The challenging part is finding our way there. When I was in early recovery, I felt extreme emotional fragility. I had spent most of my adult life developing and acting out in my addiction, so when I chose sobriety, or stopped acting out in my sexual behavior, I felt a deep loss of identity. I had no idea who my authentic self was. All I knew was that I was no longer engaging in my destructive sexual behaviors.

Sitting at the café in Berkeley, I feel overwhelmed. It has only been a week since I was discharged from treatment.

The coffee shop is buzzing with UC Berkeley students chatting and studying.

In my fragile state, I feel bombarded by the rattling of silverware, the clinking of glasses, the squeaking of chairs, the ringing of cell phones, and the clicking of computer keys. I feel faint and disoriented.

As Ellen returns with our tea, I feel the beginnings of severe nausea. Ellen, oblivious to my mood, is chatting about the excitement she has found in her recovery. She has invited me to coffee after taking me to my first Twelve-Step meeting. Her face is moving in and out of focus, her voice pounding in my head like a kid jumping on a trampoline.

Abruptly, I stand. "I have to go," I say, surprising even myself at my rudeness.

"Oh, okay," Ellen says, as if she is used to such erratic mood swings.

"How much do I owe you?" I quickly ask.

"Oh, don't worry about it," Ellen replies with a kind smile.

"Get you next time," I say, turning and heading for the door.

I breathe the October night air. Attempting to orient myself, I wonder if this is my fate in recovery. Am I going mad? Have I entered the Twilight Zone and no one has told me?

I would later discover that those feelings, responses, and visceral experiences were all part of the withdrawal phase of sexual recovery. Like any addiction, sexual addiction has a withdrawal period, a process that is just as uncomfortable as chemical addiction. In our addiction, we have literally created an IV drip or chemical cocktail as addictive as heroin.

In choosing to get sober, we pull the plug on our drug, and we must suffer the consequences of our withdrawal. The symptoms include mood swings, fatigue, headaches, nausea, changes in sleeping and eating patterns, irritability, disorientation, loss of concentration, and depression.

Ellen and others had assured me there was a better way. And so, like most addicts, when my pain outweighed the reward, I made the leap of faith. I let go of my addiction and fell into the void of my recovery. The big question was: What would fill the void?

I had learned the saying from Alcoholics Anonymous (AA), "Fake it until you make it." I came to understand that you could act your way into good feelings and that proper behavior nurtures healthy emotions. Even if good behavior does not make you feel good at first, the AA saying urges: Do it anyway. Habitual sober behavior will eventually yield self-esteem, intimate relationships, and healthy sexuality, providing you are patient.

In the childhood abuse we sexually addicted people suffered, we were forced to disconnect from ourselves. It was the result of sacrificing our authentic emotions in order to serve our immature and needy caretakers. The characteristic perversion resulting from this disconnection is that sex addicts lose the ability to get pleasure from sexual activity, even as they declare their need for sexual pleasure. In fact, they do not know what sexual pleasure is. The abuse they suffered in childhood caused them to fuse fear, shame, lack of power, and intensity with sexuality. Until addicts recover from this abuse, sexual motives will carry the rest of the painful bundle.

Recovering sex addicts will discover the use of manipulative sex to obliterate or ameliorate the fear, shame, and powerlessness wired into them by childhood sexual abuse. Emotional disconnection has caused a monumental mistranslation in which danger, intensity, fear, anger, shame, and powerlessness have come to mean "sexual pleasure."

Undoing this perversion of the emotional truth and revitalizing the addict's authentic self are the aims of recovery. During recovery, we reconnect to our authentic selves, and we recapture and experience the safety that we lacked as children. In this feeling of safety, we begin to build what I call a "congruent" self, wherein, on all levels of our being, we move toward living in the truth and take the first steps toward healthy intimacy in relationships.

So the answer to the original question—"How do I know when I am expressing myself in a healthy manner?"—becomes clear. It is when we feel emotionally safe, connected, and affirmed in the act of sexual expression. We create this connection when we act with integrity, our values and beliefs intact.

An effective way to measure whether you have reached this point is to note how you feel after you have been sexual. Is it life-affirming and positive? Or is it the re-creation of what we have known all of our lives: the feeling of shame? If your sexual expression elicits safety, love, and a feeling of emotional connection, it is healthy.

In recovery, our sexual experiences slowly become acts of affirmation and right intention, ultimately promoting an overall feeling of well-being. This is a process that takes time and patience; it provides a path into a place of sexual wellness and health.

Crawling into bed, I have feelings of hopelessness and despair. I don't believe I can take this level of pain. I want relief. I want to act out. But then I remember what one of the guys said to me in treatment. Looking in my eyes, he said, in a thoughtful, quiet voice, "Maureen, you are worth it; you can do this." I believed, in that moment, that he believed in me. With that thought, that gift from a fellow addict, I was able to believe I could do it and that I was worth it. I knew, if only for that fleeting moment, that I was going to be all right.

One Step at a Time

That's how it goes in early recovery: a minute, a step, and a thought at a time. Living in a seemingly foreign land, we begin to navigate our new life, our new selves. We learn to live with intention, a conscious life, as opposed to one of disconnection and numbing. We begin to identify what we are feeling and the sensations in our bodies.

Most people believe their sexuality is about their genitals, the stimulation, gratification, or "chase of the orgasm." Often, clients will explain sex as being so "intimate," when in reality they are describing *intensity* rather than intimacy. The more intensity or the "greater" the sex, the better the high.

Without the potential of a high, the idea of "normal" or healthy sex becomes fearful, even dreaded: "It will be boring. I will feel trapped." Addicts do not like change, nor do they like letting go of power and control—or the illusion of it, because that is how they learned to survive. However, the reality is that sex in recovery is not boring; it is just different.

Healthy sexuality is 10 percent about our genitals, while the remaining 90 percent is about our life force, our creativity, and our passion. This energy taps into the core of who we are. That's what makes this addiction so powerful, what sets it apart from all others. Our sexuality comes from the depths of our being, and so does our recovery. Examining and integrating our healthy sexual selves from this perspective results in much more than just "mind-blowing sex." It provides a spectrum of possibilities, a transformation of the whole self.

Lynn, a short woman, age twenty-five and lesbian, is four months into her recovery. She has been coming to treatment weekly because she acts out through affairs. In the beginning of treatment, she committed to a month-long celibacy contract with self and others. Lynn discovered that the idea of being sexual without the high felt foreign. Lynn had never had sex while being emotionally present, and the mere thought of it created great anxiety and fear. In her feelings of inadequacy, she decided to extend the contract for a few weeks.

"So how did your sexual encounter go with your partner this week?" I ask.

"It didn't," Lynn says, looking down and refusing to make eye contact.

"What happened?"

"Well, we started having foreplay, and then I just froze. I didn't know what to do, how to act. I felt so stupid."

Lynn sits on the edge of her king-sized bed, looking more childlike than adult. Alice, her partner of four years, has just stormed out of their bedroom, snapped on the lights in the living room, and zapped on the television to a deafening decibel level. Lynn's heart sinks. "This is not going to work," she thinks as the tears start to flow.

Determined not to give up, she tentatively approaches Alice. "Honey," she says, sitting gingerly on the chair opposite her. "Do you want to talk about it?"

"What is there to talk about? Nothing happened," Alice snaps.

"Well, at least we tried," Lynn says, still hesitant.

Alice whips her head around and stares Lynn down. "Try?" she says through gritted teeth. "You of all people know how to do *IT;* you've done it with just about every-body else but me. Maybe I am the problem, not you!"

Lynn's tears turn to sobs as she doubles over, gasping for air.

Alice knows she has gone too far. All of her pent-up anger and resentments exploded. She had wanted to hurt Lynn, to make her feel her own pain. Now she regrets it. Alice believes in the relationship, in her love for Lynn. She wants their relationship to work, but like Lynn, she is at a loss.

Early recovery brings many challenges on many levels. Lynn and Alice were able to work through the hurt and betrayal. They were able to repair the wreckage of their capsized relationship, but they needed a plan, and they needed to apply this plan one step at a time.

Because the sexual urge is the energy source of our selfhood, sexual abuse caused us to lose contact with our creative identity. In order to get back in touch with our healthy needs and wants, we have to rediscover what it feels like to be authentic, free of traumatic intimidation, and vulnerable. This reconnection will be a careful and specific process of reflection and practical exercise. It is a step-by-step process. The goal is to rediscover, in the everyday events of our lives, the healthy bond between pleasure and sexuality. Only then will it be possible to see how spiritual truths and sexual energies are connected at the highest level of our being.

As we have explored, sex addicts had to disconnect from their feelings when they were children because to acknowledge the betrayal of their parents' role of caregiver would have been overwhelmingly threatening. So they adapted, denied their feelings, and lost contact with the care and nurturing they genuinely wanted and needed.

✧ ✧ ✧ ✧

Mitchell came into treatment desperate for help. Once a successful doctor, Mitchell lost his license after violating several patients under his medical care. His addiction destroyed the work he loved and the life he worked so hard to achieve. His once-full life has been reduced to a solitary existence contained within the four walls of his efficiency apartment.

Mitchell looks at the dust covering his guitar; like a child's toy, it has sat idle for years. It was once his joy. As an adolescent, he taught himself to play and even started a band. When he reached college, he replaced the pleasure he got from the guitar with a fierce addiction to Internet porn.

Holding his guitar in his lap, he feels a familiar comfort, as pleasant memories spontaneously float through his mind. He notices a calmness that is juxtaposed with an electric excitement.

As he plucks each string, he feels exhilarated. Unlike the high of his sex addiction, this feels clean and healthy. Tentatively, he begins playing flamenco music; before he realizes it, Mitchell is transported, his fingers flying with precision. He is completely in the moment, present only in the notes and the melody he creates. He feels alive, full, complete, healthy, and whole.

Abruptly, Mitchell snaps his palm over the strings, silencing them. Painful feelings have welled up inside. But it is too late, and tears run down his cheeks. They are tears of sadness and joy, a strange combination of melancholy and hope. But he does not push them away. He lets them flow. Intuitively, he knows this is a passage to a better place, a place he is now ready to embrace.

When Mitchell reconnected with the music that meant so much to him, he had a restorative association between pleasure and self-esteem. The music and Mitchell's authentic self became congruent; they fit together as part of a force greater than him.

Mitchell is a short, slight man in his early thirties who has an intense manner. His jaw is locked, his eyes stern, and his speech clipped. On the rare occasions when Mitchell smiles, he appears controlled and distant. It is as if there is something going on in his head that is distracting him, something that is more important or interesting.

"So, Mitchell," I ask, "how did your tasks around self-nurturing go this week?"

"I didn't do them," he says, unabashed.

"Why is that?" I ask.

He looks up at me, annoyed, without responding.

This type of resistance is typical in early recovery. It is important not to shame the client for not following through; instead, he must figure out what the resistance is about.

"I think it's stupid," Mitchell says.

"Well, I can understand why it can feel trivial, but there are reasons it is important."

Male resistance to self-nurturing is a universal pattern. I remember when I gave a talk on healthy sexuality to a group of twenty recovering sex addicts. I was describing the gifts of self-nurturing, such as stimulating the senses by lighting incense or scented candles, when a large, burly man flew out of his chair.

"You've got to be kidding me," he said without even waiting for me to call on him. "There is no way in hell I am going to be lighting scented candles or incense. What are the guys going to think when they come over? The only smell I like is the smell of propane!"

Of course, he got a good laugh. He was expressing what we explored in Chapter 9: the cultural bias and homophobia that are rampant in our culture. Being sensitive, nurturing, or sensuous with yourself is not about threatening your sexual orientation or masculinity; it is about being in touch with your body and learning to pleasure it in nongenital ways.

Let's go back to our model for sexualized anger.

In our addiction, we learned to fill our shame core from the outside: how much sex we scored, how many secrets we could get away with, how large our porn collection got, how great we looked, how much attention we could solicit. These were all delusional ways we temporarily filled our emotional void.

In recovery, we learn to fill ourselves from the inside out. This is done through the arts of self-nurturing and self-care. Each time we honor ourselves by listening or supportively reacting to our internal cues, we are healing the shame core. This is the foundation of sexual health.

In her book *The Intimacy Factor,* Pia Mellody explains that self-esteem is built through self-nurturing, or the attunement of your physical, emotional, and spiritual needs and wants. By attuning and pleasuring yourself at this level, you create connection—a connection that was severed long ago.

As trauma survivors, we learned to disconnect not only from our feelings, but also from our bodies. This was how we survived. Coming home to our bodies, or being present, can feel awkward or uncomfortable. It can also generate a great deal of fear: the fear of the unknown, the fear of triggered memories, or actual physical discomfort or pain.

This is why recovery is a process, a gradual building of self-attunement and awareness. We allow ourselves to build on each step to avoid overwhelming or flooding our systems with too much change, confusion, or information. We learn to live in the moderation of recovery, as opposed to the extremes of addiction.

"So what is the reward of lighting scented candles?" Mitchell asks snidely.

"It isn't about scented candles," I say. "It's about learning what you like and integrating that into your everyday life."

"And this helps how?"

Mitchell will come to learn that, by habitually catering to his sense of pleasure, he will reawaken his sensitivity to pleasure and discover that pleasure does not accompany fear, intensity, powerlessness, and shame. He will learn that pleasure is not the reward of manipulation and control; it is something he deserves, in and of itself.

It is not a usual part of my therapy to philosophize with clients about how, at the deepest level of our being, we are vitalized and made spiritual by our erotic energy. However, as "the holder of their shame," I know that my own creativity, based in my own recovery of sexual, spiritual energy, makes me an appropriate trustee of my clients' secrets. I draw my healing power from my belief that the liberation of sexual energy is a return to the authentic self and to the Eros, which is our sexual energy.

In these modern times, sexuality has become overwhelmingly associated with genital stimulation. But it is important to understand that there is an ancient and respected tradition in which sexuality—what the Greeks called "Eros"—was a divine energy at the center of creation.

In Plato's *Symposium,* Eros is the longing inherent in the human being for the Original Source, the Creator. It is the "sexual instinct," or spirit, that drives us from the earthly realm to seek transcendent union. This erotic theme is expressed in art, dance, literature, and mysticism. The philosopher Paul Tillich described Eros as "the driving force in all cultural creativity and in all mysticism."

One commentator on the Hebrew wisdom of the Torah said:

We moderns have an almost desperate need to be in control. The rugged individualist who is captain of his fate and master of his destiny is our cultural spiritual model. And yet we know in some deeper place that we cannot always, nor is it desirable for us, to always maintain control.

The Eros of sex is the place where we learn to give up control. And a great truth is revealed to us. In the act of letting go—of giving ourselves up—in the *la petite mort* (the little death) of orgasm, we find ourselves as well. At the very moment when the self is lost, it is rediscovered in higher and more brilliant form. Sexual Eros models for us a moving beyond old contradictions. Self-control is not the sole cauldron in which self is forged. Losing control with holy intentionality becomes the place where finding higher self is a genuine possibility.

To surrender to this force of another is true eroticism, and it is, in my opinion, holy. I believe that Eros in our intimate relationships models the surrender to a higher power. But for sex addicts, who are so damaged that they have lost sight of the preciousness of their own being, true eroticism has become impossible.

Precursors to the Sexual: Little Pleasures

Buddhists believe that, to be integrated into the creative and destructive natural processes of the universe, we must learn the acceptance of suffering. Psychoanalytic and existential therapies make a distinction between two fundamental kinds of suffering. One is a consequence of fate (i.e., everyday problems such as sickness, grandiose bosses, and rambunctious children). We bring further suffering on ourselves when we try to escape it by denying its existence. If we accept the fact that suffering is part of our lives, we don't have to fight it by hiding our eyes from the truth—or from what the truth demands of us in the way of acceptance.

Therapy is an effort to open our eyes to the reality of how we have distorted our minds and emotions in order to avoid and deny painful reality. Therapy does not deny that reality can be painful; it teaches acceptance and, at its best, the joyful transcendence that comes with the recognition of a power greater than ourselves.

Making yourself into a victim, as women tend to do, or making yourself into a stoic anti-dependent, as men tend to do, is a disempowering delusion, part of an elaborate process of self-deception instigated by childhood abuse. Acceptance of suffering as part of the life of each human born of imperfect parents is a healthy recognition of the truth of the human condition. Such acceptance empowers us because it prompts us to find ways to live healthfully within that truth.

Mitchell, now three months further into treatment, looks tired and road-worn. His skin is sallow, his eyes puffy, and his expression blank.

"I don't know if I can do this anymore," he says in a defeated tone. "I'm having a hard time."

"How so?" I ask.

"It is just dragging me down."

"Have you relapsed, acted out?" I ask.

"No, no, not at all."

"Well, that is great progress. Even though you are emotionally uncomfortable, you have been able to tolerate your feelings. Congratulations."

Mitchell's anger is deep-seated. The rejection he experienced early in life made power and control the compass of his life.

It is the second of May, and Mitchell, who has crossed each date off the kitchen calendar for the past month, is well aware it is his birthday. As is tradition in his first-grade class, his mother will bring cupcakes for an afternoon party, where his classmates will play games and sing "Happy Birthday." Mitchell is a shy, small boy who has few friends. He is often teased about his thick glasses and pigeon toes. At the tender age of six, he suffers from headaches and constant skin rashes. On this day, his birthday, Mitchell believes all of this will be put aside. For at least one day out of the year, he will feel proud.

Anxiously, he watches the clock. The afternoon bell rings, signaling the start of his party. Mitchell is ecstatic. But, to Mitchell's surprise, his classmates head for the door and out to the playground, not at all interested in participating in the classroom nerd's birthday party. Some kids even grab cupcakes as they go.

"Let's get out of here. Let's get away from the weirdo," he hears them mutter under their breath. Mitchell can barely breathe as tears stream down his face.

"It was devastating," Mitchell says.

"Sounds like it," I reply. "This memory is what triggered your sadness?"

"Yeah, it just came to me when I dropped my daughter off at school. I hadn't thought of it for years. I saw this kid with a balloon on the playground and, boom, there it was, clear as a bell, like it happened yesterday."

There is grief in recovery as we remember those times when we didn't think we deserved our place on this planet. So many of us have been told that it is shameful for us to have wants or needs. Self-care becomes a shameful act. We forget that the pleasure associated with fulfilling our needs and wants is our precious birthright. Believing we deserve this becomes a daunting and seemingly unimaginable task.

Vulnerability
Learning to Be in a Relationship

The step-by-step process by which we reacquaint ourselves with healthy pleasure is part of reviving our ability to recognize what is going on inside of us. Once we can properly identify our emotions, needs, and wants, and attune to our bodies, we must learn how to communicate that truth to others. Speaking our truth with respect and listening to the truth of others with respect are the basic necessities of healthy relationships. But, because sex addicts have damaged relational skills, in self-defeat they put all sorts of blocks in the way of relationship and connection.

Because of the wounds we have endured, learning to relate is one of the most challenging tasks we undertake in our lives. As we have explored, the issue of betrayal is huge for sex addicts and so, in turn, is the restoration of trust.

Most recovering sex addicts are terrified of re-creating painful or shaming experiences. We teach ourselves to sexualize our feelings in order to buffer ourselves from being emotionally vulnerable. Sexual addiction becomes the defense against real or imagined emotional rejection.

Aware of it or not, the wounded sex addict learns to approach all potential and real relationships through the filter of his relational history. His intuition tells him that being close to or vulnerable with another is not safe. When a new person comes into his life, he will screen this person through his filter, and the message that will be relayed is: *DANGER!*

By the time sex addicts have arrived in treatment, they usually have few, if any, friends. They may have many people in their lives, but most of these relationships are based in enhancing their sex addiction.

The floors of the high school halls shine like the polished deck of a luxury yacht. The low morning light gleams from them as Mitchell makes his way to his locker. His habit of arriving early to school began years ago. The early start gives him an added edge, which Mitchell finds comforting. He usually sits on the floor, his back against his locker, reviewing or finishing his homework. He likes to imagine that the "peer-proclaimed wimp" is in control. It provides a confidence booster prior to the distress he feels when the halls stream with fellow students.

Mitchell's daydream is interrupted as he notices the signs hung by the student council the night before; brightly colored artwork lines the halls. Mitchell feels despair as he reads the announcement for the homecoming dance.

Mitchell lives in a small town in southern Indiana, a tight-knit community that demonstrates its enthusiasm and spirit through Fourth of July parades, town-hall Christmas carols, and sold-out high school sporting events. An event like this is a big deal.

"How did the dance turn out for you?" I ask.

"It was the worst," Mitchell says. "My mother, if you can believe this, set me up with this girl, who I later found out she *paid* to go—some girl from another county who didn't talk to me all night."

"Your mother probably thought she was being helpful, but that must have felt like a huge betrayal. And then add the humiliation of how your date acted," I say.

"Exactly," Mitchell says, now animated. "That really cemented my fear and distrust of women."

"Wasn't this when your addiction really took off?"

"Big time. After that, I just gave up."

Mitchell learned to hide in his addiction to porn. He learned that his shame and fear of emotional rejection far outweighed the risk of being vulnerable. Instead of living in connection and sharing his truth with another, he learned to live in reaction, behind walls of fear, anger, and resentment. This was the home of Mitchell's trauma. From this place, he could never have a relationship, much less a truly erotic one.

Like other recovering addicts working toward healthy sexuality, Mitchell must identify his fears and expectations as belonging to his wounding. He also must understand how his dysfunctional traumatized self undermines his attempts at intimacy.

This means that, if a person is going to engage with another, whether in friendship or intimacy, he has to learn how to access his needs and wants while respecting the needs and wants of his partner.

When we enter into a relationship, we strive not only for the enhancement of the self, but also for the enhancement of the relationship. When we work for the betterment of the relationship, it takes us out of our self-centered fear and out from behind the walls of aggression, defense, and retreat.

Learning boundaries is a fundamental tool in relational development. In order for our relationships to become intimate, we must learn the art of controlled vulnerability. A concept from the work on boundaries presented by Pia Mellody. Controlled vulnerability means the ability to keep yourself safe and utilize boundaries, while at the same time being vulnerable. Controlled vulnerability keeps us open enough that our partners can know us, but it defends us from destructive incoming energy.

Our bodies are made up of energy. We learned as children to become attuned to our caregivers' energy. We knew when they walked in the room what their mood was, without their saying a word. We picked up on their energy, their vibration. In fact, most of us became hypervigilant to energy; it's the way we learned to survive.

Addicts live in extremes. They flood energy like Ingrid Bergman in *Casablanca,* oozing sexual energy like thick molasses dripping off the screen. Or they are walled off, emotionally shut down like the Terminator, a robotic character void of emotional connection and authenticity.

The goal in emotional maturity is the moderate expression of our energy, neither flooding nor damming its flow. It becomes a steady stream of conscious expression.

When we practice controlled vulnerability, we protect our partners from the unloving or disrespectful energies that we, as perfectly imperfect human beings, have the potential to discharge. This is the job of our "containment boundary," whereby we protect our partners from ourselves. At the same time, we learn to protect ourselves from unloving or disrespectful energies targeted toward us. This is the job of our "protective boundary," whereby we protect ourselves from our partner's lack of containment.

Sex addicts have fears of abandonment and judgment. Their fears build unconscious expectations that their partners in relationship "make them feel" the way they do. This is called "the victim stance," and it runs rampant in our culture. We habitually blame another person or situation rather than taking responsibility for the realities we choose to create. I say "choose" because our realities and reactions are products of our personal experiences. What might upset one individual could mean nothing to another. A person's response to a certain situation or other person is determined by his or her individual experience.

For example, if every time your father beat you, a red light turned on, you became conditioned to respond when you saw a red light. You may break out in a cold sweat, your breath may become shallow, or you may panic.

Or let's say that your mother was controlling, or yelled or withheld her attention when she was upset with you. You will respond within your relationships the way you responded to her. You will react to a certain behavior, tone of voice, or other nuance that taps into your original wounding. This is why the implementation of boundaries—for both partners—becomes crucial as relationships develop.

✧ ✧ ✧ ✧

As Janet drives, she is struck by the transformation of the foliage as she ascends the mountainside. The desolate terrain gives way to a forest that stretches out like a multicolored carpet. When Janet turns the corner into downtown, she notices the yellow and crimson leaves dancing across the street, reminding her of Midwestern autumns. She is lost in her sweet memories and emotions when she is jolted out of her reverie by a sharp cry and the abrupt curling of her husband's body in the passenger seat, as if he is blocking the right hook of a prizefighter.

Shocked and upset, she yells at him: "What's wrong with you?"

His body is now poised like an animal ready to pounce. She is both surprised and curious about his erratic behavior.

"What is the matter?" she says impatiently.

"There was a car pulling out, and you didn't see it," he says with agitation, his finger pointing in the direction of the parking space.

"I saw it," she snaps back, feeling attacked and defensive.

"Well, you didn't act like you saw it," he says in an accusatory tone.

"Well, I did," she says with indignation.

Janet feels insulted and dismissed. "Does he think I am incapable of driving?" she wonders from her victim stance.

Janet takes a deep breath. She wants to unleash her anger and shame on him, but instead she takes another breath, attempting to calm herself. This is where the challenge lies in mature emotional connection. Despite how her partner has acted or how she makes herself into a victim, Janet must choose to move beyond her primal response by interrupting her knee-jerk reaction.

Janet takes another breath, securing her containment boundary with the intention of creating emotional safety within the relationship. If she released her unbridled rage, she would experience boundary failure. She would be living in the reaction to her wounding. Instead, she chooses to collect her feelings, reactions, and thoughts.

Janet chooses to respond from a mature and emotionally centered place. She will become curious about her response, as well as her partner's. She will become clear about her own history as it relates to the present moment and will invite her partner to do the same. This is where intimacy and vulnerability begin.

Each of us is a collection of experiences that, when explained, will weave a clear path to understanding, compassion, and connection in our relationships. This conscious thought and action takes a lot of energy, awareness, and willingness. It is a practiced behavior that, with continued reinforcement, becomes more and more automatic.

"What's going on? You seemed really reactive in the car," Janet says in a calm manner.

Her husband just stares back at her, seemingly lost in thought.

"Have you ever been hurt in a car accident?" she asks with more tenderness.

Pausing and seemingly surprised by the question, he says, "Yeah, I have. I took out three windshields with my head."

When Janet's husband shares his story, his body relaxes and his eyes soften. Her sense of irritation is replaced with a sense of compassion, warmth, and love.

Through our trauma, we are conditioned to personalize another's response. In reality, it is always about the other person's wounding, experiences, beliefs, and filters. To avoid the victim stance, it is vital that we learn to ask, to be curious about the other's reality. When we do, we allow for connection, and that is where intimacy exists. We need to notice the response of the other but not lose our own boundary by reacting from our wounding.

Where so many relationships land, however, is in the blame game: "You *made me* feel frightened, sad, angry, shamed, guilty," and so on.

These unrealistic accusations are the basis for the resentments they harbor, and the walls from which they attack, defend, or retreat. Because the only "self" with whom sex addicts are in contact is the wounded self, they fear that their inadequacies will be discovered if the truth is known. Because they cannot believe in themselves, they cannot trust anyone else to believe in them; if their partners knew the truth about them, they would leave them. Dysfunctional reasoning tells them to take what they want before it can be denied them.

Stages of Relationships

The fear of being discovered as defective makes sex addicts fear intimacy. The closer they move to their partners, the more vulnerable they feel. This increasing vulnerability scares sex addicts into aggressive and defensive postures.

The emotional walls addicts construct cause them to conduct their relationships in extremes. Their containment boundaries fail them, and they spew their emotions like a garden hose. Or their protective boundaries fail them, and they can become emotionally flooded, not allowing themselves to be approached or touched by any emotion or physical contact. Or they may wall themselves off so thoroughly from their own authentic emotions and the desire to be physical that they become as silent and untouchable as a tightly shut clam. Boundary practice teaches us to regulate the levels of respect, affection, and sexual intimacy that are appropriate to our relationships.

With implementation of boundaries, the development of healthy relationships can begin. In establishing or assessing relationships, it is helpful to apply the concentric circle model. This concept may be difficult or awkward for the recovering sex addict because of his limited ability to relate. To explore these levels, let's consider the diagram below.

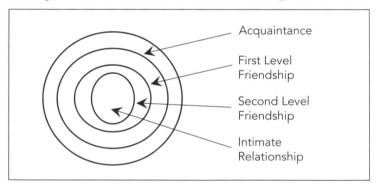

The concentric circles represent levels of relational development or emotional connection: The closer to the center of the circle, the more intimate the relationship.

The outermost region represents acquaintances, such as the clerk in the coffee shop. You are friendly with him or her but share little about your internal emotional world: "How is it going? Can you believe this weather? How about that game last night?" This emotional level allows for an amiable hello or passing exchange of niceties. The level of emotional risk is low, the exchange pleasant.

The next circle represents a first-level friendship. These relationships are deeper than acquaintanceship. This may be a new relationship you are building and perhaps assessing to determine if it is appropriate to move into a deeper emotional connection. Or it could be a long-term relationship based on shared interests, hobbies, or beliefs. You enjoy the relationship but realize your emotional connection is limited.

The second-level friendship is developed and nurtured through deep trust and emotional connection. These are confidantes who have established mutual respect and are committed to the continual growth of the relationship. These friendships are very similar to an intimate relationship minus the sexual connection.

An intimate relationship reflects the emotional connection of a second level-friendship but includes a physical component. These are committed relationships between potential or lifetime partners. These relationships are nurtured at the deepest levels.

The circle and its levels can be adjusted for individual needs. For example, your levels of friendship may be more defined; an added level or levels may feel more appropriate within your internal construct. The levels are also fluid; a person who is an acquaintance may progress into a second-level friend, or someone with whom you have a more intimate relationship may shift to an outer level. Life circumstances—such as a move, a shift in job responsibilities, an illness, or the birth of a child—may dictate a change in connection to another person.

I invite the sex addict to assess each relationship and where it falls within this continuum. You may realize that one level is deprived, whereas other levels are overflowing. As in all aspects of recovery, the goal is balance. Hopefully, this exercise will assist in the conscious assessment of your connections to others and in the enrichment of their development.

Relational closeness may feel overwhelming to the recovering sex addict because the threat of emotional exposure is no longer masked by sex. Learning to be present, authentic, and honest is part of the learning curve in developing healthy relationships.

❖ ❖ ❖ ❖

The room is crowded, with all members of group in attendance. The energy seems low, perhaps due to the tender issues being explored. The usual banter is absent, replaced by a somber mood.

It is Mark's turn to share with the group. His assignment was the exploration or visual representation of his addiction. He has made a collage and, as he unrolls the large butcher-block paper, I am immediately struck by the sparse images spread before us.

"This is my addiction," Mark says with little enthusiasm.

"Tell us about it," I say.

He begins with a litany of meandering thoughts, like blood leaking from a loose tourniquet that fails to arrest the bloodbath that has occurred. Making little eye contact, Mark limply points to the pasted images: "This picture of tornado damage represents the damage caused by my addiction; this money represents the money I have spent on my addiction."

The group's feedback is equally benign: "It sounds like you worked hard on this. Good job. Thanks for sharing."

"Okay, Tim," I say to the last group member to give feedback. "Now tell him what you really think."

Tim looks at me with fear in his eyes, as if to say, "Let me skate through this; I am not in the mood for a challenge."

"Are you willing to be real with Mark instead of sugarcoating it?" I ask.

Tim looks up at Mark, making brief eye contact and then quickly lowers his head like a racer guilty of a false start. Taking a deep breath, he looks straight into Mark's eyes, this time holding contact.

"I just can't buy this, man," he says, gesturing toward the collage. "I mean, for me, my addiction was dark, dangerous, ruthless. I mean, ready to destroy. I think you are holding back," Tim continues, courageously positioning himself in a vulnerable emotional exchange.

"Why do you think Mark would hold back?" I ask Tim.

"Well, I know for me it was the shame. I couldn't show this stuff to anyone."

"What was it like when you finally did?"

"I felt really good, you know, a relief," Tim continues, seeming to have found his stride. "I really want to get to know you, man; that's why we're here. I'm not here to judge you. I've been there."

"How does that feel, Mark, to hear that from Tim?"

"It feels good," he says, still walled off.

"Mark," I say, pushing his comfort zone. "I want you to respond with what is really going on for you."

Taking a deep breath as if garnering strength, he looks up at Tim: "I guess this is all new to me. I don't know; thanks for what you said."

"Mark, I want you to dig deeper. How does this feel?" I ask.

"It's different, you know, scary for me. I'm afraid if I show who I was in my addiction, you are all going to run away, and I can't say I'd blame you."

This may be the first authentic moment Mark has had in a very long time. This is the beginning of authentic connection. A pivotal turning point in his recovery, being real and intimate is a courageous step toward healthy sexual connection on all levels.

Intimacy with a New Partner

When sex addicts move into a more intimate relationship, they must slow down the process. I recommend seventeen dates spread over at least three months before genital contact. During that slow courtship, the recovering sex addict has time to practice the habits of self-esteem and boundaries that he has learned in therapy and in group.

This courtship period at first involves boundaried communication, emphasizing the pleasures involved in being honest and respectful. I urge clients to use talking and listening boundaries because this kind of connection creates safety and trust. The recovering individual is implying, "I trust you. I am willing to be open to you. I trust myself enough to trust you."

For most sex and love addicts, sex has always equaled power and control, something other than connection. So entering love in this way is a whole new experience for a sex addict because he is being present. And being present can be terrifying.

Once you are developing good communication skills, learning who your partner really is, and knowing your own needs and wants, you introduce physical but nongenital expressions of affection and love.

Activities might include massages, holding hands, snuggling, rubbing each other's back, and washing each other's hair; this allows a connection to the physical. You want to take what you enjoy and share that with your partner. And your partner will do the same.

Learning relationship skills, meaning boundaried behaviors, is hard enough. So how does a recovering sex addict share, during the boundaried interchange, that he or she has behaved in destructive, unethical, immoral, and harmful ways?

If you are starting to date a new person, you want to share in broad strokes. You don't want to get into the details, but you do want him or her to know that you have issues around your sexuality that are based in your trauma. Go into detail only to the level of what appears appropriate to you. You must trust your sense of authenticity.

Before you do this, do a practice run with your Twelve-Step sponsor or therapist. Have it scripted out. Talk about it in group and with other people who have done it.

Prepare yourself before the event with your support people and afterward share with them what the experience was like for the two of you. By doing so, you are connecting in a healthy way, and you are supporting yourself in doing something that is terrifying for sex addicts.

Some kinds of sexual acting-out histories are particularly risky to talk about because they are so blatantly condemned by society. Bestiality is one example. Here is a scenario of how such a fraught discussion might proceed:

"I'm really enjoying your company, and I really want to move into a more committed relationship with you, and be with you exclusively. But there are some things that I want to share with you so that you will know who I am and where I am coming from. I think this will bring us closer in our relationship. In the past, I have had some issues around my sexuality. Those issues began when I was a child when my family was highly sexualized and did not have appropriate boundaries around sexuality. And so I learned that sex was my most important need. That's where I was valued. That's where the power and attention were. That moved me into some unhealthy behavior as an adult.

"Now I am going to therapy and am in a group in order to deal with these issues. I am not currently active in these inappropriate behaviors. I am active in is what *we* are experiencing right now. But I want you to know this about my past, and I want you to ask me any questions that you need to for clarity. I don't want to go into the details of it right now, but I do want you to know who I am now."

Let us say the response you get is polite but wary. It might sound like this:

"I appreciate your honesty. What I have heard is that you come from a sexually unhealthy and overactive family and that damaged you. Now you are getting treated for it, and I am grateful for that. But I have some fear around this. Do you think you are well enough to go out with me? I mean, what are you talking about? You say that you don't want to go into the details now, but trust me with the details. Why are you withholding from me? Do you trust me?"

"I do. But the problem is that I don't necessarily trust myself. I still have a lot of shame about what I am dealing with, and I haven't done this before. And I want to do this right."

"You know, I really hear you. And from what I know about you, that's great. I feel very warm toward you."

That's the nice scenario. But let's say her response sounds like this:

"You know, this is not the first time that I have heard something like this. When you decide that you want to be honest with me, give me a ring. Meanwhile, I have some thinking to do."

We may conclude that the recovering addict does not have the right partner. At this point, at least you know the truth and have created an appropriate place to stop investing in the relationship. You are slowing down that process to find safety for yourself and for the relationship if you think it is worth pursuing.

Even though this painful scenario is not far-fetched, my clients who are walking the path of recovery usually find that honest intimacy in communication has good results.

✧ ✧ ✧ ✧

Hank, a thirty-ish committed bachelor, has been in therapy for more than a year. Through the years, he has learned to defend his emotional core with a gruff, intimidating exterior. His full-body tattoos, heavy-metal jewelry, leather jacket, motorcycle boots that match his Harley, and his deep voice and bulging muscles send the message: "Don't mess with me."

Hank recently began dating a woman named Sara; it's the first exclusive relationship of his life. He is heartily embraced and is implementing healthy relationship tools: boundaries, communication skills, being real, staying in touch with his feelings, and getting reality checks from his support groups.

A few weeks into his relationship, Hank called the office between appointments, asking for clarification and support.

"I need to check something out with you," he began. "I got together with Sara last night, and she started to rail on me, how I was being an asshole."

"What caused that reaction?" I asked.

"We were out having a steak, and I ran into a buddy of mine. I started talking to him and, the next thing I know, she's shooting me the death look. You would have thought I was hitting on some chick," he said. "So I did that bubble thing, the boundary, you know, what we worked on last week: putting an energy field around me, protecting myself. Is that what I am supposed to do?"

"You got it," I said in an affirming tone. "How did that feel?"

"Felt good, safe. I liked it."

Hank's willingness to implement the relationship skills he is learning demonstrates his commitment to recovery. The building of new skills can often feel tedious, awkward, and uncomfortable. But the results of one's efforts can be gratifying.

"What happened after you finished your conversation with your friend?"

"I checked it out with her, and she came clean about how she was feeling left out, jealous. So it was cool."

As the weeks passed, Hank's relationship progressed into a deeper connection.

"I think I need to tell her about my past—you know, all the sex stuff," he said. "But I am not sure how to do it."

Fear was written all over Hank's body as he made this suggestion. The idea of being vulnerable and risking rejection is one of the most difficult challenges that recovering sex addicts face. The concept of being accepted and valued despite their past behaviors is so foreign and unimaginable that they can barely visualize it, much less believe they deserve it.

When Hank told Sara about himself, he began by explaining his sex abuse history, laying the foundation as to why his life had taken its particular course.

Hank began by explaining that his father, an ex-amateur wrestler, beat him, especially when he was drunk. His mother left when Hank was three, never to be seen again. He later found out she had been killed in a car accident when he was seven. His father regularly took him to bars, where Hank was exposed to his father's drunken stupors and carousing.

"I hated those times," Hank explained to Sara.

"My dad was so loud and obnoxious. Even though the place was a dump, I got embarrassed. He'd pick up women, often more than one a night, and either had sex with them in the pickup or brought them home and had sex right in front of my brother and me," Hank said, pausing to collect his thoughts.

"My sex addiction started early. . . ."

In the middle of Hank's sentence, and much to his surprise, Sara reached out to touch his hand.

"I really admire you, Hank," she said with tenderness. "I know this is hard for you, and I feel really special that you are willing to share this with me."

Hank now shakes his head as he relays the story: "It's a freaking miracle."

Hank had been willing to be vulnerable, and the results were an even deeper connection with Sara. He had picked someone who was willing to accept his past and believe in his future.

Hank was able to experience a common occurrence for sex addicts in recovery. When we are on the healing path and doing our work, we tend to attract people who match our healthy energy. It is a simple equation, like energies attracting. Hank was doing the work and reaping the benefits. He began to realize he was now the navigator of his life, able to chart his course. He was making choices and decisions that allowed him to experience true intimacy and relational connection.

Existing Significant Relationships

Repairing existing relationships is another focus of healing. If you are in recovery, chances are your partner is aware of your addiction; it is probably the reason you entered treatment. He or she found receipts, e-mails, videos, or computer images, or received a call from an angry sex partner, disclosing the lurid details of your acting-out behavior.

Your partner was devastated, shocked, enraged, and desperate. There were threats of suicide or homicide, accusations, name-calling, ultimatums, disbelief, and questions—so many questions.

You were shocked by the intensity of your partner's reaction. Witnessing your partner's gut-wrenching pain and anger was like staring at the carnage of your addiction. It was a reflection of the darkest parts of your addiction and the unimaginable places you allowed it to go.

You tried to explain, manage, apologize, make promises, implement change, or take actions to amend, but nothing seemed to help. Your partner's reaction was continuous, emotional waves so unpredictable that you felt like a boat being ravaged by a turbulent sea.

Like your wounding, the betrayal cut your partner to his or her core. The deepest parts of his or her personhood were violated, probably a reflection of your partner's own trauma history. He or she needs to be angry to process the betrayal, and this process must be respected.

The reality is that this process is difficult, even when it is carried out in a boundaried, healthy fashion. For a person who does not have an understanding of the recovery process to receive such painful, intimate information can result in an excruciating loss of control. And although this loss of control can precipitate a crisis, there is good news: The crisis can create such desperation that the sufferer becomes ready to learn a new, healthier way to cope with the situation.

This crisis is like that of alcoholics who get "sick and tired of being sick and tired." They know the next drink will kill them, but they can't live without it. They reach bottom as the crisis confronts them with all its awful might. With great good fortune, they may finally be ready to accept help.

There is always the possibility, although it is less likely, that your partner is unaware of your addiction. He or she is choosing to live in denial or knows something is "off" but is unwilling to explore the reasons. Your partner has developed his or her own coping mechanisms that serve to distract. These can include work, overscheduling, exercise, overeating, and overspending.

In these cases, a disclosure will be necessary to begin the healing process. Disclosures may also be needed when the partner is only partially aware of the addict's behaviors. He or she may have found online porn but may be unaware of the addict's anonymous sexual encounters.

I have rarely conducted a disclosure wherein the partner did not have some inkling that the other partner was indulging in some clandestine and perverse behaviors that were betraying the relationship. Very rarely have the offended parties been shocked and had no prior knowledge. Usually they had seen the symptoms, but they had ignored them.

Disclosures are not meant to hurt the partner, but rather to begin the process of relational repair. If secrets exist on either side of the relationship, healthy connection is not possible.

I have often been challenged or questioned about disclosures in relationship to the ninth step of the Twelve Step model, which states that the recovering person has "made direct amends to such people wherever possible, except when to do so would injure them or others." Making a disclosure is never pleasant, but, if it is done in a manner that supports both partners, the result is not "harm;" it is feelings of pain, which are real and necessary to acknowledge.

Pain is a healthy and necessary element of the healing process; it allows growth and awareness. To avoid feelings, or the possibility of feelings, is to avoid recovery.

Telling the truth in a supportive boundaried manner with the intention to heal a relationship may bring up such feelings as pain, fear, shame, or guilt. The expression of these feelings in your partner my be painful to witness; however, the disclosure is not intended to injure them, but rather to allow for the truth to be revealed.

It is important to follow a specific plan when making disclosures in a respectful manner, ideally in a therapeutic setting that supports both partners. Often addicts jump the gun or are insensitive to their partners' needs. They may have difficulty knowing what to say or how to say it. They may have good intentions, but, in their haste to disclose, they reveal too much, perhaps without offering any emotional support. They may tell only part of the truth, attempting to control or ease the blow, and then "leak" information that prolongs their partner's pain.

Once the disclosures are made, the reconstruction can begin. Communication and boundary practice will be the most important aspects of early relational repair. Vital activities include scheduling couple and family check-in times, doing feeling checks, giving and receiving affirmations, focusing on what is right or working in the relationship, and learning to voice and meet each other's needs and wants.

Early relationship repair begins by focusing on the individual issues and how those dysfunctions are being played out. Ideally, both partners are seeking individual and couples therapy. They are looking for support groups that can lend insight into their healing process. During the period of sexual abstinence, it is important to connect through activities that promote trust, partnership building, and fun, such as hiking, golf, or bridge. It also is important to schedule date nights with the focus on a relaxed, stress-free environment.

I invite both partners to take a time-out from genital contact, a period of abstinence. The goal is to allow anger, resentments, and betrayal to heal. The reintroduction of genital connection will take place over a period of time and with a specific plan.

You can then move into nongenital connection, which can include cuddling, caressing, massaging, hand-holding and kissing. Integrating what you have learned through individual attunement and nurturing is the first step in nongenital contact. It involves expressing your needs and getting to know your partner. This slows down the process, allowing each partner to be present and attuned to the other. This can feel awkward, but, the comfort level will most likely increase when this process begins.

Genital Pleasure

In the stage leading up to genital sex, you have been delaying gratification, which is extremely difficult for recovering sex addicts.

The groundwork has been laid for genital sex. The slow relational work and in-the-moment physicality have been safely and trustingly shared. You will talk to your partner about moving into the genital sex stage. Your conversation might sound something like this:

"You know that I feel closer and closer to you, and I want to share with you the experience of the physical aspect of our sexuality. And I want to introduce some of the stuff that we have already been able to do together. This involves creating pleasure, not only genitally, but throughout the whole body, the senses, and the environment we create. So I was thinking that, the first time we are sexual, we could bring some of the techniques we have used into the room with us and allow them to be present as we start to make love."

Another scenario might proceed differently as one partner shares:

"I am really scared. I have a lot of fear about having sex with you because I have never experienced sex with someone I really care about. I think it is going to be really different, but not only am I scared, I am really excited."

"You know, I really hear what you are saying. And I am excited about it, too," the partner says.

When both parties have agreed to genital contact, the sexual experience will be much different than it was during the addiction. Hopefully, the restored trust, attunement to one's body, use of boundaries, and communication skills will allow for a loving exchange that results in feelings of comfort, safety, warmth, and love. The results will be shame-free and life-enhancing, a very new experience for the addict. This will begin the restoration of genital fulfillment, an ongoing process of exploration. It can be not only new and challenging, but fun as well.

The Good News

It is paramount in recovery to accept *your* own process. We all do it differently. I witness over and over how sex addicts tend to compare their progress in recovery to others. This is born out of the shame of their wounding at the core of their addiction. It is vital that they become aware of this propensity to judge and measure and then learn to intervene on this self-destructive pattern. This intervention is vital to the early stages of the recovery process because, if we continue to "beat ourselves up," we fuel the shame that drives the addict. If we continue to engage in self-destructive and judgmental thoughts, we are in jeopardy of relapse.

It is fundamental to understand that *your* healing process is as unique as your fingerprint. It is yours to honor. I support my clients in reciting and internalizing the affirmations and slogans from Alcoholics

Anonymous: "Progress, not perfection," and "Easy does it." These simple messages tend to have a soothing effect on shame, like a cooling balm on an infected wound. The simple and humble truths of these statements provide a refuge from the barrage of habitual, self-demeaning, destructive judgments with which our addict has attacked us for so long.

We tend to heal as we were wounded. The earlier, more pervasive, intense, and repetitive the abuse, the longer it can take to heal. A natural response to threat or danger is to recoil or constrict. The more intrusive the wounding, the tighter we recoil. The challenge in early recovery lies in the ability to allow internal, healing vitality to take over. We were born with a storehouse of good health and joy, but we have been out of contact with it for so long. This is a huge challenge for most addicts because it requires us to let go and trust. Letting go can cause over-whelming feelings of anxiety: "If I let go, I will get hurt. I might die."

It is important to acknowledge these old beliefs and to challenge their treachery. When anxiety attacks us, there are practical things we can do: prayer, self-affirmation, exercise, controlled breathing, a telephone call to our sponsor. These things work.

I often share with my clients that recovery is a "process, not an event." This process requires patience and acceptance. It is vital to celebrate and honor all accomplishments, great and small. Your recovery is unique and precious. The gifts of this process are reflected in the promises of all Twelve Step work:

"If we are painstaking about this phase of our development, we will be amazed before we are halfway through. You will know a new freedom and a new happiness. You will not regret the past, nor wish to shut the door on it. We will comprehend the word 'serenity,' and we will know peace."

Chapter 11

CHISELING OUT YOUR SOUL

To know and live in a place of peace is the hope I hold for my clients. However, the path of recovery can often feel treacherous and full of steep slopes, crags, and ravines. In Alcoholics Anonymous, there is a metaphor that likens the recovery process to peeling back the layers of an onion. As we gain access to the center, we gain deeper understanding and we clear the way for growth.

Riding the highs and lows of recovery can also feel like a roller coaster. Sometimes the rising path feels limitless, exciting, and clear, while the descent evokes an overwhelming sense of despair and disorientation. This is the nature of the healing process.

It is important to understand this process because, in the beginning, there can be great elation, as you find you are able to quickly gain insight, resources, and support around recovery. You are developing new awareness as old paradigms shift and new ones emerge. It is as if the world has gone from black-and-white to color. Everything becomes clearer and more enriching; there is hope and promise. This period is called the "pink cloud," and it is a time in which you experience discovery, personal awareness, a sense of gratitude, and motivation. The path is clear, and the answers come easily.

When the "pink cloud" bursts, elation is replaced with a cold dose of reality. The process no longer feels effortless; it is tedious and arduous. Often the client wants to stop recovery or may be vulnerable to relapse.

Recovery is the restoration of the soul. This deep process may seemingly have a life of its own, an unspoken agenda that you have been invited to join. The journey is more intuitive than intellectual, more feeling than thinking, more being than doing, more releasing than controlling. It is a journey that feels counterintuitive to all that your adapted self has taught you about yourself and about life. That's where the challenge lies; it's where, if courage prevails, victorious results are realized.

I have mentioned twelve-step groups throughout this book, and I believe they are very helpful to recovering sex addicts. The Twelve-Step model for sexual addiction was born out of the Twelve Steps of Alcoholics Anonymous. However, the focus and language involve sexual issues. The twelve steps of Sex Addicts Anonymous are:

1. We admitted we were powerless over addictive sexual behavior—that our lives had become unmanageable.
2. We came to believe that a Power greater than ourselves could restore us to sanity.

3. We made a decision to turn our will and our lives over to the care of God as we understood God.

4. We made a searching and fearless moral inventory of ourselves.

5. We admitted to God, to ourselves, and to another human being the exact nature of our wrongs.

6. We were entirely ready to have God remove all these defects of character.

7. We humbly asked God to remove our shortcomings.

8. We made a list of all persons we had harmed and became willing to make amends to them all.

9. We made direct amends to such people wherever possible, except when to do so would injure them or others.

10. We continued to take personal inventory and, when we were wrong, promptly admitted it.

11. We sought through prayer and meditation to improve our conscious contact with God as we understood God, praying only for knowledge of God's will for us and the power to carry that out.

12. Having had a spiritual awakening as the result of these steps, we tried to carry this message to other sex addicts and to practice these principles in our lives.

The *Sex Addicts Anonymous Book* explains the importance of working through the twelve steps:

These steps are the heart of our program. They contain a depth that we could hardly have guessed when we started. As we work them, we experience a spiritual transformation. Over time, we establish a relationship with a Power greater than ourselves, each of us coming to an understanding of a Higher Power that is personal for us. Although the steps use the word God to indicate this power, SAA is not affiliated with any religion, creed, or dogma. The program offers a spiritual solution to our addiction, without requiring adherence to any specific set of beliefs or practices. The path is wide enough for everyone who wishes to walk it.

The first step on the path is often the most difficult, because the idea of going to a meeting of strangers to disclose your most shameful behavior and thoughts is often unimaginable. The gift of a twelve-step program is the reduction of shame. When you walk into a room and share your story and hear others, you might, for the first time in your life, feel relief from the grasp of your addiction. Instead of people running away from you, horrified by your past, they embrace you and invite you into their healing circle. This experience can be a spiritual moment because of the possibility of transformation and hope.

The Twelve-Step model can also challenge sex addicts' core beliefs. The group holds addicts accountable by requiring them to work the twelve steps, and it can function as an addict's first "healthy family," accepting them unconditionally. Such groups help addicts by mirroring, supporting, and affirming them as they move toward sober and healthy sexuality.

When addicts share their experiences, strength, and

hope, individuals do not sit in judgment or call them perverts. Rather, people say, "I identify with you." As shame is lifted, individuals move into a better position; they are less defensive and can begin to look at their cognitive distortions and other coping mechanisms. Self-esteem will undo addiction; just as abandonment fuels shame and shame fuels addiction, healthy self-love fuels connection, which is the base or glue of spirituality.

The Twelve-Step program says that healthy self-love is the basis of recovery. It states: "Having had a spiritual awakening as a result of these steps," addicts learn that they are not terminally unique, and this reduces the sense of shame that is at the core of all sex addicts. This is the gift of humility. Addicts recognize their own humanness, which allows the emergence of the true self.

At the heart of the Twelve-Step model is spirituality. Addicts are challenged by the twelve steps to admit their powerlessness, to develop a relationship with a power greater than themselves, and to turn their will and lives over to this higher power. The goal of the steps is to allow addicts to see how their choices about their behaviors are not working, that they are not in control, and that they need help.

However, the mere language of the twelve steps—"letting go, turning it over, surrendering"—is enough to make an addict flee a twelve-step meeting. Being in control, or having the illusion of control, is how he survived. "Surrender" translated into shame, abandonment, fear, or death. The addict closed off his internal world as if he were cast away on a deserted island. Having no needs or wants, he learned to sustain emotional deprivation and even take pride in the lack of sustenance. Holding onto control or the illusion of control provided a false sense of security.

The transformation of recovery comes about with a realization: The only things you have control over are your choices, *not* the outcomes. It is a huge moment in recovery when an individual realizes that he needs help, and that, through letting go of control, change is possible.

The addict who is involved in individual and group therapy, as well as a twelve-step program, has a better chance of maintaining sobriety. One reason for this success rate is the enormous impact that twelve-step meetings can have on challenging the addict's cognitive distortions.

Cognitive distortions are thought patterns or defenses that protect us from our pain. Because these defenses operate from the unconscious, the individual is often unaware of them until his beliefs and attitudes regarding change are challenged. The irony is that, even though defenses protect the addict from his pain, these same defenses are the obstacles that stand in the way of recovery. For addicts, even considering discarding their defenses is extremely frightening because it leaves them vulnerable to feeling pain.

Spiritual Development

The spirituality of recovery is about healing the wounds of abandonment and disconnection. A baseline definition of spirituality is connection: with self, with others, with life at large, and with a power greater than yourself. Within this backdrop of connectedness, spirituality, as it relates to healthy sexuality, necessitates the reconnection with self. This then allows for the possibility of healthy sexual connection with others. The act of self-discovery is at the center of recovery.

When we emerge from sexual dysfunction into health, we are like a sculptor who sees, in a formless block of marble, the shape of something beautiful and desired. When we work on ourselves, we chip away at what has hidden our beauty and desirability from view. As Stephanie Urbina Jones sings: "I am chiseling out my soul like Michelangelo. Found my spirit in the stone, I am chiseling out my soul."

If we are to be the artist of our personhood, we must first connect to the fullness of who we are. Because of our traumatic histories, we have been entombed; we need to break out from that which blocks the expression of our capacity for relational intimacy, so that we can connect to our partners and to a power greater than ourselves.

Michelangelo released the figures entombed within the marble; the sculptor liberates the image latent in the stone. That liberated image is what we often call "the authentic self." The authentic self is the precious gift of who we are, restored to us by chiseling out the soul from its entombment in trauma-induced sickness.

A second image comes from a novelty shop in Florence, Italy. The shop sells replicas of Michelangelo's unfinished sculptures. The caption on the bottom reads, "Be patient; God isn't finished with me yet." This tells us that the search for self is a process and that chiseling the soul is the artistic goal of the spiritual life.

Putting It into Practice

Jacob, a man in his mid-fifties, is a retired engineer whose training taught him to solve problems and implement change with precision, allowing no margin for errors.

"When I was in graduate school, all I did was study," Jacob explains. "I had no social life, no friends. I ate, slept, went to class, and studied; that was my life."

"What was that like for you, to live that way?" I ask.

"I didn't have a choice; if I wanted to get through school, I had to work for my grades—not like my roommate, who was a natural."

"It must have been lonely."

"It didn't matter. I wanted to graduate."

"You sound like you were determined."

"Let me explain how it was," Jacob continues. "The tests were basically equations we had to solve, like if you were an engineer and this was the equation for the bridge you were building. The calculations had to be correct; there was no margin for error. Otherwise, the bridge would collapse; anything less than 100 percent was failure."

Jacob had been in therapy and group process for six months. He had been struggling with the concept of spirituality and was often confused, offended, and frustrated by the abstract idea of something greater than himself. His frustrations were often demonstrated by outbursts of anger and pain.

"You know, I need proof," Jacob began one night during a group discussion.

"I need proof that this stuff is real. If you can give me some empirical data, then I might be able to buy into this stuff. But, otherwise, I'm not buying it."

"I have no proof," I said.

"Then I can't buy it," he snapped. "You know I want to get it," he continued, his anger melting into tears of frustration. "I really do," he said, his voice trailing off.

Jacob was struggling with a concept beyond his grasp. Everything he been taught intuitively and intellectually was counter to what he was hearing. He was scared to let go of what he knew. If it was incorrect, like an incorrect equation for a bridge, his world would come crashing down.

Jacob was unable to tolerate the blending of the concrete, comprehended by intellect, and the spiritual, apprehended by faith. Without the willingness to explore and integrate the physical, emotional, and spiritual aspects of the self, Jacob cut himself off from the miracle of recovery. He locked himself into the painful reality of his status quo.

Jacob left treatment shortly after our group meeting. His tears demonstrated his inner conflict between the familiar ramparts of his rigid intellectuality and his defiance and fear of spiritual uncertainty. I believe that the bridge that leads to the world of spiritual connection leads us to our sense of preciousness. Jacob was unwilling or afraid to cross it.

We need to trust in the preciousness of ourselves, which allows us to recognize the preciousness in others. And then we need to trust in a power greater than ourselves, which binds humans together in a community of love or, at least, respect. Without this trust, we cannot begin to chisel away at the defenses of dysfunctional adaptation, which hide our true and precious beings—our authentic selves.

On the spiritual level the barrier against entry becomes most powerful. The hold of the mundane world is strong. The doubts in our intellectual minds have contempt for the mysteries of higher truths. But our trust in a higher power creates the possibility of connection with forces greater than ourselves. These forces give us the serenity to believe that we belong in the universal order. Through faith, we become *a part* of the beneficent operation of the universe, rather than *apart* from it.

That inner knowing can then develop into a sense of congruence with the world. That sense of belonging, of feeling "at home," gives us the optimistic energy to perform our best work. For the first time in our lives, we feel that we are among friends. Our lives become conscious expressions of our fitness to be alive and healthy; we experience being present in a world that cares for us.

To live this blessing, we must be restored to wholeness; we must recover our preciousness so long buried beneath the rubble of our wounding. We must bring together all of the recovery tools we have begun to use in therapy. These tools include the ability to know our emotional fears or blocks, the ability to communicate our needs and wants, and the willingness to be vulnerable and to share respectfully our knowledge of ourselves with our partners.

Sexuality is at the heart of our life force. It is our creative urge, and it is not expressed only through sexually explicit acts. Because our sexuality is so linked to the essence of who we are, it is inexplicitly interwoven into our spirituality. Healthy sex supports the awakening of our soul, our inner knowing and truth. It opens the possibility of deeper connection with others. This does not mean that the spiritual connectivity of sexual intercourse is memorable only because it is uplifting. It is also memorable because it is intensely pleasurable. When we willingly and consciously enter the act of lovemaking, we offer our precious humanity to the care of our partners, and we accept our partners' offer of their precious humanity for our own safekeeping. That is an awesome act of spiritual communion, and a responsibility not to be taken lightly. To betray it would plunge us sex addicts back to where we were when we were first betrayed, when we were taught that love and betrayal were the same thing.

The Divine

Surrendering our intellectual defenses in the search for spiritual meaning can be threatening. Spiritual development, enhancement, and practice require a balance between the rational and the intuitive. The rational guides our steps along the road to emotional recovery; the intuitive opens us to the possibilities of connection to and through a higher power.

We are often unconscious of divine energy in our daily lives. Ben, a homosexual in early recovery, was working on this very issue. He told me, "I want intensity in my sex life; I want excitement. I have no idea what you're talking about when you talk about a spiritual connection."

I suggested to Ben that spiritual connection existed in many things of which he was already aware, such as great music, dance, food, and nature. I suggested he spend some time in the natural settings that he loved. I suggested he quiet himself, take everything in, and see what happened.

"I tried the exercise," Ben reported the following week. "I went up to the reservoir. You know, they have a path that is three miles long. The only thing I noticed was the bare-topped men jogging," he explained with a smirk.

Despite Ben's resistance and lack of belief, he persevered. Each week, he returned with a similar story. It wasn't until the sixth week that he changed.

"You know, the most profound thing happened at the reservoir this week. It was late in the day, so it was quiet, and I was climbing this hill when I heard a rustling noise. I looked up, and I saw the leaves of this aspen tree dancing in the breeze. The sun illuminated them from behind, and it looked so magical. I stopped and stood there for a good five minutes. I was captivated by the beauty."

Ben had experienced a connected moment, which allowed for transformation and tranquility. It was a moment of deliverance for Ben, a deliverance from the bondage of addiction, disease, and darkness. Once awake, Ben's awareness surfaced often.

"I saw the most tender scene last week," Ben reported a few weeks later. "I was sitting at the coffee shop, and a little boy about three years old approached a graying golden retriever. He was unafraid; the boy walked straight up to the animal and extended his hand. The dog struggled but rose to his feet. The boy backed away a few steps but allowed his hand to remain outstretched. For a few moments, both stood silent with locked eyes. And then the dog took one gentle step and lovingly licked the boy's fingertips. A slow smile emerged on the boy's face. It was a beautiful moment." he sighed.

Graceful moments surround us. Grace is a gift of divine energy given to us as an affirmation of our belonging. It tells us we have a safe home.

We do not force it or will it to happen. When we stop and open ourselves to connection, grace abounds. And when grace abounds, we are well. As we heal from our wounds, we become more sensitive to the universal energies around us, and we vibrate with spiritual connection. The recognition of our congruence with spiritual connection is the greatest gift of living. In recovery, it is our responsibility to reclaim that gift.

RESOURCES

Resource List

Adult Children of Alcoholics (www.adultchildren.org)
310-534-1815

AIDS/HIV HOTLINE (Spanish) 800-344-7432

AIDS/HIV HOTLINE 800-342-2437

Al-Alateen (www.al-anon.org/alateen.html)
757-563-1600

Al-Anon (www.al.alon.org) 800-344-2666

Alcohol & Drug Referral Hotline 800-252-6465

Alcohol & Drug Information 800-729-6686

Alcoholics Anonymous (www.alcoholics-anonymous.org)
212-870-3400

Anorexia Nervosa and Associated (Eating) Disorders
(www.anad.org) 847-831-3438

Childhood Help's National Child Abuse Hotline
800-422-4453

Co-Dependents of Sex Addicts 763-537-6904

Co-Dependents Anonymous (www.ourcoda.com)
602-277-7991

Cocaine Hotline 800-662-HELP

Cocaine Anonymous (www.ca.org) 800-347-8998

Co-Anon (www.co-anon.org) 520-513-5028 Tucson, AZ

Crystal Meth Anonymous (CMA) 213-488-4455

Dakota, an extended care facility for sexual compulsive
    behaviors 800-632-3697

Debtors Anonymous (www.debtorsanonymous.org)
    781-453-2743

Drug Abuse Info, Treatment (National Institute of) 800-662-4357

Eating Disorders Anonymous (EDA)
    (www.eatingdisordersanonymous.org)

Emotions Anonymous (www.emotionsannonymous. org)
    651-647-9712

Families Anonymous (www.familiesanonymous.org)
    800-736-9805

Gamblers Anonymous (www.gamblersanonymous.org)
    213-386-8789

Hepatitis (liver) Hotline 800-223-0179

Incest Survivors Anonymous 562-428-5599

Marijuana Addicts Anonymous
    (www.marijuana-anonymous.org) 212-459-4423

Mellody House, Extended Care for Trauma
    800-632-3697

Mothers Against Drunk Driving (MADD) 800-438-6233

Narcotics Anonymous (www.na.org) 818-773-9999

Obsessive–Compulsive Anonymous (OCA)
    516-739-0062

Overeaters Anonymous (www.oa.org) 505-891-2664

Pills Anonymous 212-874-0700

Rational Recovery 800-303-2873

Recovering Couples Anonymous
    (www.recovering-couples.org) 510-663-2312

Runaway & Suicide Hotline 800-621-4000

Runaway (National) 800-421-4000

S-Anon 615-833-3152

Sex & Love Addicts Anonymous (www.slaafws.org)
   781-255-8825

Sex Addicts Anonymous (www.sexaa.org) 713-869-4902

Sexual Compulsives Anonymous (www.sca-recovery.org)
   800-977-4325

Sexually Transmitted Diseases Hotline 800-227-8922

Survivors of Incest Anonymous 410-282-3400

Students Against Destructive Decisions (SADD)
   508-481-3568

Tough Love (www.toughlove.org) 800-333-1069

Workaholics Anonymous 510-273-9253

Additional Resources

The Safer Society Foundation Inc.

P.O. Box 340

Brandon, VT 05733-0340

Phone: 802-247-3132

www.safersociety.org

Addicted to Sex (documentary)

Sean McFarland

2129 Ocean Avenue #6

Santa Monica, CA 90405-2235

Phone: 310-572-5496

Internet Behavior Consulting Company

Elizabeth Griffin, MA, LMFT

6542 Regency Lane—Suite 208

Eden Prairie, MN 55344-7848

(952) 210-5778

(952)-903-9257 (fax)

www.internetbehavior.com

Hermes Web
Marketing office:
10120 Hage Drive
Corcoran, MN 55374
Phone/Fax: (763) 498-7464
sarah.techau@hermesweb.com
www.hermesweb.com

Society for the Advancement of Sexual Health (SASH)
P.O. Box 725544
Atlanta, GA 31139
(O) 770-541-9921
(F) 770-541-1566
sash@sash.net

Harry Benjamin International Gender Dysphoria Association
  (HBIGDA)
1300 South Second Street
Minneapolis, MN 55454
(O) 612-624-9397
(F) 612-624-9541
hbigda@hbigda.org

Association for the Treatment of Sexual Abusers (ATSA)
4900 West Griffith Drive Suite 274
Beverton, OR 97005
(O) 503-643-1023
(F) 503-643-5084
www.atsa.com

INDEX

A

abandonment 12, 44, 54, 89, 91, 93-4, 100-1, 125, 129, 133, 230, 259
  fear of 16, 129
  molds 16
abstraction 68
abuse 11-2, 15-9, 35-40, 43, 68-9, 78-80, 87, 89, 93-4, 133, 144, 146-7, 160, 196-8, 200, 202-3, 214
  abusers 43, 79, 87, 119, 125, 128, 155, 173, 198
  alleged 197, 200
  children 109, 122, 171, 200, 224
  covert 36, 57
  definition of 35
  emotional 12, 49, 180
  imagined 16
  mother's 57, 128, 171, 185
  overt 35, 44, 94

L

M

R